INTRODUCING
MICROSOFT®
.NET

David S. Platt

PUBLISHED BY
Microsoft Press
A Division of Microsoft Corporation
One Microsoft Way
Redmond, Washington 98052-6399

Library of Congress Cataloging-in-Publication Data
Platt, David S.
    Introducing Microsoft.NET / David S. Platt.
       p. cm.
    Includes index.
    ISBN 0-7356-1377-X
    1. Internet Programming.   2. Computer software--Development.   I. Title.

  QA76.625 .P54 2001
  005.2'76--dc21   2001030139

Printed and bound in the United States of America.

1 2 3 4 5 6 7 8 9   QWE   6 5 4 3 2 1

Distributed in Canada by Penguin Books Canada Limited.

A CIP catalogue record for this book is available from the British Library.

Microsoft Press books are available through booksellers and distributors worldwide. For further information about international editions, contact your local Microsoft Corporation office or contact Microsoft
Press International directly at fax (425) 936-7329. Visit our Web site at mspress.microsoft.com. Send
comments to *mspinput@microsoft.com*.

Acquisitions Editor: Danielle Bird
Project Editor: John Pierce
Technical Editor: Marc Young

Body Part No. X08-04509

To my daughter,
Annabelle Rose Platt

Contents

Chapter Five

Windows Forms 177

Epilogue and
Benediction 199

Foreword

I first met David Platt back in 1998, when I was thinking about writing a book about COM. The potential editor for my book had also edited Platt's *COM and ActiveX Workbook* and gave me a copy to look over so that I could see "what we've published before." I found it to be a remarkable and very detailed book. (OK, I didn't really meet Dave in the flesh, but reading a book by someone is just like meeting them, except different, of course.)

Skip ahead a few years (and one book on COM and DCOM never written because of illness), and I find Dave in my office here at Microsoft, this time in the flesh. By now I've also had a chance to read his excellent text on COM+ and many of the chapters you are about to read. This was the chance I'd been waiting for! I wanted to know whether he was as funny and interesting as his latest writings. Indeed he is, but with more hair.

Dave's writing style has changed from his earlier writing. His COM+ book, as well as this one, are cheeky and fun to read. They are almost a different genre of book. I know what you are thinking: "*Genre? This is a computer book.*"

You see, I was thinking about the taxonomy of programming books the other day, and I've noticed three types:

- The hardcore type, with lots of code; a book that usually covers one particular subject. Dave's book on COM and ActiveX falls into this category. These books answer the question *how*.

- The in-depth type that offer a very deep analysis of a system, with quite a bit of code. Don Box's COM book is an example of this type. These books answer the question *why*.
- The mind set book. This type provides a high-level and easy-to-understand overview of a subject, with some code. However, these books don't try to give you an exhaustive look at everything, like the first category, nor do they try to go into the very deepest crevices, like the second type. Instead, their intent is almost metaphysical: they try to give you the Zen of their subject. These books teach you when to ask *how* and when to ask *why*.

Introducing Microsoft .NET is definitely an example of the last kind of book. It's funny to read and very informative, with lots of interesting code. But it's really about teaching you the mindset of .NET. And trust me, there's a mindset switch. You'll need to think in a new way to become a .NET wizard. It's not all that hard, and the book you hold in your hands is the first step.

Keith Ballinger
Program Manager, .NET Framework
Microsoft Corporation

P. S. I've often wondered whether people read the foreword. If you're this far, help my research and send me an e-mail: *keithba@microsoft.com*. I'll reply with the results so far.

Preface

I always thought that the product now named Microsoft .NET sounded very cool. I remember reading Mary Kirtland's articles in the November and December 1997 issues of *Microsoft Systems Journal* describing what was then called COM+, a run-time environment that would provide all kinds of useful services, such as cross-language inheritance and run-time access control, to object programmers. As a COM geek, I liked the way this environment promised to solve many of the problems that kept hanging me up in COM.

Microsoft then decided that the next version of Microsoft Transaction Server would be called COM+ 1.0 and would be integrated into Windows 2000; what Mary had described would be COM+ 2.0. Later, Microsoft renamed COM+ Microsoft.NET, and I coined the term MINFU, Microsoft Nomenclature Foul-Up, for all this jumping around. But the product still sounded cool, and I was thrilled when Microsoft Press asked me to write a book about it with the same high-level treatment as I had given COM+ 1.0 in *Understanding COM+* (Microsoft Press, 1999). You are holding, and, I hope, buying, the result.

I was afraid that Microsoft wouldn't let me tell the story my own way, that they would insist that I hold to the party line. That didn't happen in this book, not even once. Everything that I say in this book, whether you agree or disagree with it, is my own call. Obviously, I like .NET and think it will make its users a heck of a lot of money, and Microsoft doesn't disagree. When a prospective employer asks you for a reference, do you provide someone who thinks you're a demigod, or someone who thinks you're a turkey?

Most programmers I know could provide some of both. In some internal correspondence about an early draft, a project manager took exception to one of my rants about administrative tools and wrote to me, "it makes the purpose of the book more editorial than instruction, IMO. Is that your intention?" I wrote back to this person, "I am proud that my book points out the bad parts of .NET as well as the good, the costs as well as the advantages. I'd be a weasel if I did anything else. IMHO, I consider this to be instruction. If you're accusing me of calling 'em as I see 'em, I plead guilty, as charged."

I can't stand dry reading, any more than I can stand eating dried-out fish or meat. I remember my freshman year in college, when I tried to spice up a chemistry lab report with a couple of jokes and got flunked for my pains. "Levity has no place in science," my professor said. "Do it over again. Passive voice should be used throughout." He's the only guy I've ever met with a mustache carefully shaved into a permanent frown. You didn't get tenure, did you, Phillip? Lighten up, you'll live longer, or at least enjoy it more. Maybe he was trying to keep himself bored to make life *seem* longer, but he shouldn't take it out on the rest of us.

To me, the best authors are also the best storytellers, even in, or especially in, the often dry fields of science and history. For example, I greatly admire Laurie Garrett's *The Coming Plague* (Penguin, 1995), Evan S. Connell's *Son of the Morning Star* (North Point Press, 1997), and William Manchester's biography of Winston Churchill entitled *The Last Lion* (Little Brown, 1983). Think about your college textbooks, written by people like my former professor. What could be a bigger turnoff? Then read this excerpt about Emile Roux's development of diphtheria antitoxin and the first human trials, during a vicious outbreak in Paris in 1894:

> Roux looked at the helpless doctors, then at the little lead-colored faces and the hands that picked and clutched at the edges of the covers, the bodies twisting to get a little breath....

Roux looked at his syringes—did this serum really save life?

"Yes!" shouted Emile Roux, the human being.

"I don't know—let us make an experiment," whispered Emile Roux, the searcher for truth.

"But, to make an experiment, you will have to withhold the serum from at least half of these children—you may not do that." So said Emile Roux, the man with a heart, and all voices of all despairing parents were joined to the pleading voice of this Emile Roux.

You can read about Roux's choice and its results in *Microbe Hunters* by Paul de Kruif, originally published in 1926 and periodically reissued, most recently in 1996 by Harcourt Brace. Not much academic objectivity there, but which would you rather read? I know which I'd rather write. I do not come close to de Kruif's eloquence, and I seriously doubt that anyone will be reissuing this book when I'm 112 years old. But I've done my best to make it slide down easily, and how many technical authors even try?

De Kruif closes his book by saying, "This plain history would not be complete if I were not to make a confession, and that is this: that I love these microbe hunters, from old Antony Leeuwenhoek to Paul Ehrlich. Not especially for the discoveries they have made nor for the boons they have brought mankind. No. I love them for the men they are. I say they are, for in my memory every man jack of them lives and will survive until this brain must stop remembering." As I say in my epilogue (no fair jumping there now; you have to read the whole book first), the Internet is doing nothing more nor less than evolving the human species. Microsoft .NET is the product that's going to crack it wide open. And I find it extremely cool to be chosen to tell the story and to tell it my own way. To talk with the project team, to discuss what the future of computing will be and why, is the reason I switched to Microsoft Press from my former publisher. Early readers have told me that comes through in my text. I certainly tried for that, and I hope they are right.

Every book is a team effort, like a moon launch but on a smaller scale. The authors, like the astronauts, get such glory as there is (you're all coming to my ticker tape parade, aren't you?), but without all the other people who worked so hard on this project, you'd never get to read it. Like the thousands of Project Apollo team members, most of them get very little acknowledgment (although I think the chain-smoking, vest-wearing flight controller Gene Kranz, played by Ed Harris, nearly stole the show from Tom Hanks's Jim Lovell in the movie *Apollo 13*.) Until someone makes *Introducing Microsoft.NET* into a movie (a fine idea, any producers out there?), I'm afraid they're stuck with only this acknowledgment to tell the world of their deeds.

First honors must go to John Pierce, the lead editor on this book. He played a secondary role on my last Microsoft Press book, *Understanding COM+*, a couple of years ago. I was very happy to find out that he was available for the lead role on this book. His sense of humor is as warped as mine. Hiring him to keep me in line is like hiring Bill Clinton to chaperone a high-school girls' cheerleading squad. I knew he wouldn't cramp my style or change my voice, which, love it or hate it, you'll have to agree is distinctive. He shaped my prose in a better way than I could have.

Next comes Marc Young, the technical editor. He tracked down the answers to all of my technical questions, usually under great time pressure and in the face of daily changes to the code builds. In addition to Marc, many of the .NET project development team took time from their brutal schedules to set me straight on things. I'd like to especially thank Susan Warren, Keith Ballinger, Mark Boulter, Loren Kohnfelder, Erik Olson, John Rivard, Paul Vick, Jeffrey Richter, and Sara Williams.

On the acquisition side, Ben Ryan started the process a year ago, and Danielle Bird took over when he moved on. Anne Hamilton backstopped the process. Teresa Fagan, a Microsoft Press group product manager, upon hearing the working title *Introducing Microsoft .NET* had the idea, "Hey, you ought to get that as a web address," and I ran through the rain back to my lonely writer's garret (OK, it was the Bellevue Club Hotel's concierge floor) and snagged it before anyone else could act on the thought. That was the cherry on top of the sundae.

I'd also like to thank Duane Baker and Chris Bell of Interland, Inc., for working with us to set up the Web site where you can see demonstrations of the sample programs in this book.

Finally, I need to thank my wife Linda, now a mother to our daughter, Annabelle.

David S. Platt
www.rollthunder.com
Ipswich, Massachusetts, USA
April 2001

```
        'PROBLEM: This procedure is required by the WebServices ...
        'Do not modify it using the code editor.
        InitializeComponent()

        'Add your own initialization code after the InitializeComponent
        'call.
    End Sub

    Private Sub InitializeComponent()
        'CODEGEN: This procedure is required by the WebServices Designer
        'Do not modify it using the code editor.
        components = New System.ComponentModel.Container()
    End Sub

    Overrides Sub Dispose()
        'CODEGEN: This                                          ...esig...

#End Region

<WebMethod()> P...                              ...yVal ShowSec...
                                                As String

If '...
```

Chapter One

Introduction

I cannot get my sleep to-night; old bones are hard to please;
I'll stand the middle watch up here—alone wi' God an' these
My engines, after ninety days o' race an' rack an' strain
Through all the seas of all Thy world, slam-bangin' home again.

> —Rudyard Kipling, writing on the importance of 24/7
> availability under load, "McAndrew's Hymn," 1894

The Big Internet

The Internet is Big. (Annoyed Reader: "I paid you HOW MUCH
to tell me that?" Royalty-Counting Author: "What, you mean, it's
NOT?")

On its own, a desktop PC is boring, much as a single-cell amoeba
is boring. Sure, you can use it (the PC, not the amoeba) to play a
mean game of Solitaire and it won't let you cheat (this is an advantage?), and Notepad comes in handy on occasion. But unlike
the evolutionary value of the amoeba, the economic benefits to
society of the stand-alone desktop PC have yet to be satisfactorily
proven. It just can't do that much interesting or useful stuff as long
as its horizons remain limited to its own box. However, when you
use the Internet to link your PC to every other PC in the world,
and to every intelligent non-PC device (palmtops, refrigerators,
and so on) as well, for essentially no extra hardware cost, fun
things start to happen—just as when enough single cells connect
and evolve to form the human brain, which can compose, play,
and appreciate a symphony; fly to the moon; or obliterate its own
species. Beats the heck out of Solitaire, doesn't it?

Stand-alone PCs are
much less useful than
networked PCs.

The Internet continues to change society ever more rapidly.

The Web started out as a means for browsing boring physics reports and took off (understatement of the century) from there. It dramatically lowered the friction of distributing all types of data. Expanded content attracted more users to the Internet, and the increasing numbers in the audience drew in more content providers in a virtuous cycle that not only shows no signs of ending but is accelerating even as I write these words. Yesterday I used the Web to watch video highlights of a hockey game that I missed. After that, I used Napster to find some good music among 500,000 different songs (I only look at the legal ones, naturally) on 10,000 different users' hard drives. Then I talked to my mother about setting up a video camera link so that she could look into her first grandchild's crib from her home 500 miles away. The Internet has made ours a completely different world from that of even five years ago.

Internet hardware and bandwidth are cheap and getting cheaper.

Hardware for connecting to the Internet and bandwidth for transmitting data are cheap and getting cheaper. The Web camera that lets my mother watch my daughter cost only a couple of hundred bucks to install in my PC and essentially nothing extra to operate over my existing cable modem. Think what it would have cost ten years ago, or even five, to buy video hardware and lease a dedicated line from Ipswich, Massachusetts, to Orwigsburg, Pennsylvania. The prices of Internet hardware and bandwidth will soon fall to Cracker Jack prize level, if they haven't already.

Raising the Bar: Common Infrastructure Problems

Internet software poses new classes of problems that are difficult and expensive to solve.

The hardware and bandwidth are cheap, but there's a snag. Platt's Second Law states that the amount of crap in the universe is conserved.[1] If someone has less crap to deal with, it's because he's

---

1. Platt's First Law is called "Exponential Estimation Explosion." It states that every software project takes three times as long as your best estimate, even if you apply this law to it.

managed to dump his ration on someone else's head, but there's no such thing as making it disappear. If hardware and bandwidth are so much easier and cheaper to get, that means writing the software to run that environment must, by the laws of the universe, be harder and more expensive by a corresponding amount. And so indeed it has proved to be, as anyone who's tried lately will confirm. The problem in your Internet application isn't the business logic, which is much the same as a desktop case (a certain number is less than zero, indicating that your checking account is overdrawn). However, the fact that you're implementing an application on different boxes connected by the Internet introduces new classes of problems, because of the Internet's public, uncontrolled, and heterogeneous nature. Think how (relatively) easy it is to handle a toddler in your own living room. Then think how much harder it is to handle that same toddler in Grand Central Station. Same kid, same goals (safety, fun), entirely different requirements.

Consider the question of security, for example. Many users keep their personal financial records on stand-alone PCs, using Quicken or similar products. Developers of early versions of Quicken didn't write any security code. They were comfortable, or more properly, their customers were comfortable, that if they kept their PCs physically locked up, no one would steal their money. Paranoid users could buy a product that would password-protect their entire PC, but hardly anyone did this.

Desktop applications generally didn't have any security at all.

But Quicken on the desktop wasn't that useful, as many users discovered once the novelty wore off. It did very little more than what your paper check register already did—often more quickly and more easily than the silly program. Quicken didn't become a net benefit to users until it could connect to the Internet and allow interaction with other financial parties, with features such as electronic bill receipt and payment and automatic downloading of bank and credit card statements. (That is, it would become a net benefit to users if its user interface wasn't so lame. It doesn't handle the complexity of these new features well at all, overwhelming the user with far too many indistinguishable choices at any given time. But that's not an Internet problem.)

However, once Quicken's operations leave the secure cocoon of the single box on which they're running, they run smack into a massive new need for security. For example, when the user tells the electronic bill paying center to write a check to the phone company, the bill paying center needs to ensure that the request comes from the genuine owner of the account and not from the phone company desperately trying to stave off bankruptcy by advancing itself a couple of months' worth of payments. We also need to encrypt all the data that flows between the parties. You don't want your neighbor's geeky teenage son using a packet sniffer on your cable modem line to see your account numbers and what you bought—"$295 to Hunky Escort Service, eh? Wonder if her husband knows about that?"

This security code is extremely difficult to write—and to test, and debug, and deploy, and support, and maintain, while employees come and go. You have to hire people who know everything about security—how to authenticate users, how to decide whether a user is allowed to do this or that, how to encrypt data so that authorized users can easily read it but snoopers can't, how to design tools that administrators can use to set or remove users' security permissions, and so on.

Internet computing raises other similar classes of problems, which I'll discuss later in this chapter. All of them share the characteristic that, as I first explained in my book *Understanding COM+* (Microsoft Press, 1999), they have nothing whatsoever to do with your business process, the stuff that your clients are paying you to get done. Instead, these problems relate to infrastructure, like the highway system or the electric power grid, the framework on which you and other people weave your day-to-day lives.

Developing infrastructure kills projects. I have never seen a project fail over business logic. You know your business process better than anyone else in the world; that's why you're writing software to assist it. But you don't know the infrastructure (unless that's your product, as it is for Microsoft). Almost no one is an expert on security authentication algorithms or encryption. If you try to write that code yourself, one of two things will happen. You'll either write a lame implementation because you don't know what you're doing (and you had better hope no bad guys notice it), or you'll try to write an implementation and fail to complete it before the money runs out. When I worked on a pre-Internet distributed foreign exchange application twelve years ago (also described in *Understanding COM+*), we did both.

Infrastructure, not business logic, is what kills projects.

The Best Laid Plans

Software developers always begin a project with the best of intentions and the loftiest of promises. Like an alcoholic heading to a party, we swear that we'll avoid bugs through careful design and that we'll document our code thoroughly. We'll test it all the way through, and we won't add features after the code freeze. Above all, we'll make realistic schedule estimates and then stick to them. ("That operating system feature doesn't do exactly what we want, but I can write a better one in a week, so there's no need to modify our program requirements.") A robust, useful application (sobriety) is within our grasp, all we have to do is stay disciplined. No Solitaire at all. At least not until after five. OK, one game at lunch. "Dang, I lost; just one more to get even, OK? Hey, how'd it get to be 4:00?" Every single project I've ever seen has begun with this rosy glow.

Software developers delude themselves.

Has anyone ever done it? Has any developer ever kept these promises? No. Never has, never will. We know in our hearts that we're lying when we promise. It's a disease. Like addicts, there's only one way out (not counting dying, which everyone does at exactly the same rate: 1.000 per person.) To write successful Internet applications, we of the software development community need to do what people in recovery do and embrace at least two steps on our path to righteousness:

1. Admit that we are powerless—that our lives have become unmanageable.
2. Come to believe that a power greater than ourselves can restore us to sanity.

You can't afford to build infrastructure yourself.

Application programmers must admit that we are powerless over Internet infrastructure. It makes our projects unmanageable. We cannot build it; it takes too long, it costs too much, we don't know how. We must not even try, for that way lies sure and certain doom. In the extremely unlikely event that we ever do write decent infrastructure code, our competitors who don't will have long since eaten our lunches, and breakfasts and dinners besides. You don't build your own highway to drive your car on, nor do you install your own power generating equipment (unless you live in California in early 2001).

Fortunately, your Internet application's infrastructure requirements are the same as everyone else's, just as your requirements for highways and electricity are similar to those of many other people. Because of this large common need, governments build highways and power companies build power plants, which you use in return for a fee, either directly through tolls and bills, or indirectly through taxes. Governments and utilities reap large economies of scale because they can hire or develop the best talent for accomplishing these goals and because they can amortize the development effort over many more units than you ever could.

You want someone else to build it and for you just to use it.

What we really need is for someone to do for distributed computing what the government does for highways (maybe not *exactly* what the government does for highways, but you get the basic idea). As recovering addicts believe that only the power who created the universe in which we compute can restore their lives, so developers need a higher power in computing to provide our Internet infrastructure, restoring our development efforts to sanity.

What the Heck Is .NET, Anyway?

That's what Microsoft .NET is—prefabricated infrastructure for solving common problems in Internet applications. Microsoft .NET has been getting an enormous amount of publicity lately, even for this industry. That's why 5000 rabid geeks, crazed on Jolt Cola,[2] converged on Orlando, Florida, in July 2000. Not because they can't pass up a bargain off-season airfare, even if it's not somewhere they want to go, or because they enjoy punishing heat and sunstroke. It was to hear about Microsoft .NET for the first time.

Microsoft .NET provides prefabricated infrastructure for solving the common problems of writing Internet software.

Microsoft .NET is an add-on run-time environment that runs on the Windows 2000 operating system. Later versions of .NET will probably be made part of the operating system, the U.S. Department of Justice willing. Later versions may or may not be announced to allow at least portions of it to run on other versions of Windows or, as we shall see, perhaps for other operating platforms as well. Microsoft .NET provides the following services, all discussed later in this book.

- The .NET Framework is a run-time environment that makes it much easier for programmers to write good, robust code quickly, and to manage, deploy, and revise the code. The programs and components that you write execute inside this environment. It provides programmers with cool run-time features such as automatic memory management (garbage collection) and easier access to all system services. It adds many utility features such as easy Internet and database access. It also provides a new mechanism for code reuse—easier to use and at the same time more powerful and flexible than COM. The .NET Framework is easier to deploy because it doesn't require

.NET provides a new run-time environment, the .NET Framework.

---

2. It's rumored that, as part of the penalty ordered by Judge Penfield Jackson, Microsoft will henceforth be allowed to serve only caffeine-free, diet Jolt Cola at its conferences.

registry settings. It also provides standardized, system-level support for versioning. All of these features are available to programmers in any .NET- compliant language. I discuss the .NET Framework in Chapter 2.

.NET provides a new programming model for constructing HTML pages, named ASP.NET.

- Even though intelligent single-use programs are on the rise, most Internet traffic for the near- to middle-term future will use a generic browser as a front end. This requires a server to construct a page using the HTML language that browsers understand and can display to a user. ASP.NET (the next version of Active Server Pages) is a new environment that runs on Internet Information Services (IIS) and makes it much easier for programmers to write code that constructs HTML-based Web pages for browser viewing. ASP.NET features a new language-independent way of writing code and tying it to Web page requests. It features .NET Web Forms, which is an event-driven programming model of interacting with controls that makes programming a Web page feel very much like programming a Visual Basic form. ASP.NET contains good session state management and security features. It is more robust and contains many performance enhancements over original ASP. I discuss ASP.NET in Chapter 3.

.NET provides a new way for Internet servers to expose functions to any client, named .NET Web Services.

- While generic browsers will remain important, I think that the future really belongs to dedicated applications and appliances. The Web will become more of a place where, instead of data being rendered in a generic browser, a dedicated client (say, Napster, for music searching) will make cross-Internet function calls to a server and receive data to be displayed in a dedicated user interface or perhaps without a user interface at all for machine to machine communications. Microsoft .NET provides a new set of services that allows a server to expose its functions to any client on any machine running any operating system. The client makes calls to the server using the Internet's lowest common denominator of XML and HTTP. A set of functions exposed in this manner is called a .NET Web Service. Instead of sitting around waiting for customers to see the light and embrace the One True Operating System (Hallelujah!), the new design seems to say, "Buy our operating system because we provide lots of prefabricated support that makes it much easier to write applications that talk to anyone else in the entire world, no matter what or where they're running." I discuss .NET Web Services in Chapter 4.

- A dedicated client application that uses Web Services needs to provide a good user interface. A high-quality interface can provide a much better user experience, as the dedicated interface of Microsoft Outlook is better than the generic Web user interface of Hotmail. Microsoft.NET provides a new package, called .NET Windows Forms, that makes it easy to write dedicated Windows client applications using the .NET Framework. Think of Visual Basic on steroids, available in any language, and you'll have imagined the right model. I describe .NET Windows Forms in Chapter 5.

.NET provides Windows Forms, a new way of writing rich client applications using the .NET Framework.

- Finally, no Internet programming environment would be complete without some mention of database access. Most Internet programs, at least today, spend most of their time gathering information from a client, making a database query, and presenting the results to the client. .NET provides good support for database operations using ADO.NET. Although I don't discuss this technology in this book, I've provided a chapter about ADO.NET that you can download from the book's web site, *www.introducingmicrosoft.net*.

ADO.NET provides good support for database access within the .NET framework.

About This Book

Until I wrote *Understanding COM+*, all of my books had been low-level how-to manuals and tutorials, with the samples written in C++. This worked beautifully for hard-core programmers who write in C++, but unfortunately this is a small percentage of the people who buy computer books, which made my creditors very unhappy. I wanted to make this book accessible to developers who didn't know or didn't like C++. Furthermore, I found that managers got essentially nothing out of my C++-based approach because they never worked with the sample programs (with only one exception I know of, and I'm sending him a free copy of this book for working so hard to understand my last one). I really wanted to reach that audience, even more than programmers. An ignorant (or worse, half-educated) manager is an extremely dangerous beast. Eliminating that species would be my grand contribution to civilization.

Sample programs and installation instructions are available on this book's web site.

This book uses the basic style I experimented with in my last book, in which I adapted the format that David Chappell used so successfully in his book *Understanding ActiveX and OLE* (Microsoft Press, 1996): lots of explanations, lots of diagrams, and very little code in the text descriptions. As much as I liked David Chappell's book, I still felt hungry for code (as I often need a piece of chocolate cake to top off a meal of delicate sushi). I found myself writing code to help me understand his ideas, much as I wrote equations to understand the textual descriptions in Stephen Hawking's *A Brief History of Time*. (OK, I'm a geek.) So my book comes with sample programs for all the chapters, some of which I wrote myself and some of which I adapted from Microsoft's samples. These sample programs are available on this book's Web site, which is *http://www.introducingmicrosoft.net*, naturally. Managers and architects will be able to read the book without drowning in code, while code-hungry programmers will still be able to slake their appetites. I wrote the sample code in Visual Basic.NET, despite all the noise about C#, because that's the language that most of my readers are familiar with. If you want to run the sample programs, you'll need a computer running Windows 2000 Server, the beta version of the Microsoft .NET SDK, and the prerelease version of Visual Studio.NET. Detailed system and installation requirements for the sample programs are available on the Web site.

Each chapter presents a single topic from the top down. I start by describing the architectural problem that needs to be solved. I then explain the high-level architecture of the infrastructure that .NET provides to help you solve that problem with a minimum amount of code. I next walk you through the simplest example I can imagine that employs the solution. Managers may want to stop reading after this section. I then continue with a discussion of finer points—other possibilities, boundary cases, and the like. Throughout, I've tried to follow Pournelle's Law, coined by Jerry Pournelle in his "Chaos Manor" computing column in the original *Byte* magazine, which states simply, "You can never have too many examples."

Each chapter of this book presents a single topic from the top down.

Warning: Prerelease Software

Contemporary software is the fastest-changing field of human thought that has ever existed. The fundamental tradeoff in writing a book on cutting-edge software is accuracy versus timeliness. If you wait to start writing until the software actually ships, the book appears on shelves six months to a year after the software does. That's often half the product's lifetime or more. Conversely, if you start writing too early in the development process, the final release of the software bears little resemblance to what the book describes. I've always tried to delay writing a product's functional spec until after the product ships; it's the only way I can ensure that the product matches the spec.

It's difficult to choose exactly the right time to write a software book.

I wrote this book in the first quarter of 2001, using a Beta 2 release of the Microsoft .NET Framework and Visual Studio.NET. I guarantee, with absolute certainty, that some features and operations will change between this writing and the actual release of the software—new features might be added, scheduled features removed, operation of existing features modified. Furthermore, when I project the course of the product's development as it moves toward release or wish for a new tool or feature, I'm speculating on my own behalf, not committing Microsoft to produce it or even to consider it. If you want to stay current with my thoughts about

I wrote this book in early 2001, using a beta version of .NET.

.NET and hear about updates to this book, subscribe to a copy of my free newsletter, *Thunderclap*, available on my Web site, *www.rollthunder.com*.

When you read this book, you'll no doubt say at certain points, "Golly, Platt is completely right [or wrong]; I wish Microsoft would change this or add that." Microsoft would like to hear from you so that they know what you want. For example, in Chapter 3, I explain that according to the current plans, Microsoft is planning to have you use Notepad to configure ASP.NET. I go on to explain why this just won't work for real administrators in a production environment. If you agree with me and think that it needs fixing, submit your thoughts to Microsoft. We'd all like to hear from you, at any stage of the development process.

Sing a Song of Silicon

Modern poetry sucks.

Modern poetry bores me silly. I find most of it indistinguishable from pompous politicized prose strewn with random carriage returns. It has no rhyme, no rhythm, just an author (usually with a private income or taxpayer's grant, else he'd starve to death) who suffers from the fatal delusion that he has Something Important To Say. Maybe my feeble mind just doesn't want to make the effort of parsing his intentional dislocations. Don't know about you, but I've got other things to do with my few remaining brain cycles.

Rudyard Kipling's poetry is great.

On the other hand, I love older poetry, especially Rudyard Kipling. He's not politically correct these days—read his poem "The White Man's Burden" if you want to know why. In his defense, I'll say that he was a product of his times, as we all are. And he won the Nobel Prize for Literature in 1907, so someone must have liked him then. My grandparents gave me a copy of his *Just So Stories*. My parents used that book to read me to sleep, and it was one of the first books I learned to read myself. I graduated to Kipling's poetry in high school English class, where I found reading his section of the literature book far more interesting than listening to the teacher. His poems still sing to me as no one else's ever have, before or since.

What does this have to do with computer geekery, you ask? The incredible acceleration of technological innovation in the last few years brings to my mind Kipling's poem, "McAndrew's Hymn," published in 1894. Most of us think of modern times as different from a hundred years ago and nowhere more so than in technology. Still, I'm astounded at how much of McAndrew's feelings resonate with me today. The title character is an old oceangoing Scottish engineer musing on the most brilliant technological accomplishment of his day: the marine steam engine. That was the beginning of the death of distance, a process that you and I, my fellow geeks, will complete ere we rest. I like this poem so much that I've started every chapter with an excerpt from it. You can read the whole thing on line at *http://home.pacifier.com/~rboggs/ KIPLING.HTML*. You may think of Scotty on *Star Trek* as the prototypical Scottish engineer, but I'm convinced that Gene Roddenberry based him on Kipling's McAndrew.

Kipling wrote a poem celebrating a marine engineer named McAndrew, almost all of which applies to programmers today.

Every programmer, for example, knows Moore's law, right? It says that computing power at a given price point doubles every eighteen months. Many programmers also know its reciprocal, Grosch's law, which states that it doesn't matter how good the hardware boys are because the software boys will piss it away. A few even know Jablokow's corollary, which states simply, "And then some." But McAndrew figured this out a hundred years ago, way before some plagiarist stuck Moore's name on the idea and called it a law. I think of Kipling's words as I contemplate the original 4.77 MHz IBM PC (with two floppy drives and 256 KB of memory) that I use as a planter:

The poem includes an early formulation of Moore's Law.

> *[I] started as a boiler-whelp when steam and [I] were low.*
> *I mind the time we used to serve a broken pipe wi' tow.*
> *Ten pound was all the pressure then - Eh! Eh! - a man wad drive;*
> *An' here, our workin' gauges give one hunder' fifty-five!*
> *We're creepin' on wi' each new rig - less weight an' larger power:*
> *There'll be the loco-boiler next an' thirty mile an hour!*

Like Rodney Dangerfield, we geeks yearn for respect and appreciation. Society has looked askance at us ever since the first cave-geek examined a sharp stone and said, "Cool fractal patterns. I wonder if it would scale to spearhead size?" Remember how girls in high school flocked around football players, most of whom (not all, Brian) were dumb as rocks? A straight-A average was uncool (mine would have been if I'd had one), and even my chess championship trophy couldn't compete with a varsity letter. Even though I knew that in the long run I'd make far more money than the high-school jocks (which my father pointed out is far more attractive to the opposite sex), it still burned. McAndrew cried aloud for the same thing, only far more eloquently (my emphasis added):

> *Romance! Those first-class passengers they like it very well,*
> *Printed an' bound in little books; but why don't poets tell?*
> *I'm sick of all their quirks an' turns-the loves an' doves they dream-*
> **Lord, send a man like Robbie Burns to sing the Song o' Steam!**

"Lord, send a man like Robbie Burns to sing the Song o' Steam!"

No Robbie Burns am I, and not even my mother likes hearing me sing. But I've done my best to tell the story as I see it today. I hope you enjoy reading it.

Chapter Two

.NET Objects

To match wi' Scotia's noblest speech yon orchestra sublime
Whaurto-uplifted like the Just--the tail-rods mark the time.
The Crank-throws give the double-bass; the feed-pump sobs an' heaves:
An' now the main eccentrics start their quarrel on the sheaves.
Her time, her own appointed time, the rocking link-head bides,
Till-hear that note?--the rod's return whings glimmerin' through the guides.

> —Rudyard Kipling, writing about the vastly different types of
> components that any large application needs to work
> together harmoniously, "McAndrew's Hymn," 1894.

Problem Background

Good code is hard to write. It's never been easy, and the problems that developers need to solve to produce useful applications grow ever more complex in today's distributed, heterogeneous Internet world. I sometimes catch myself longing for the good old days, when software development meant writing an input processor that read characters directly from the keyboard and parsed them into recognizable tokens to be fed to a command processor. It doesn't work that way any more. There are several hard problems dogging the efforts of developers today.

Good code is hard to write.

First, we have the ongoing controversy over which programming language to use. While in theory any language can produce binary code that takes advantage of the entire operating system, it's all too common to hear something like, "Hey, you're using COBOL, so you can't have automatic memory management. Get

We need all system features to be available to programmers in any language.

yourself a real language, kid." We'd like the choice of language to be dictated by how well it matches the problem domain, not by how well it matches the system features. We don't want any more second-class citizens. What's probably going to be the downfall of the Java language is that you can only use its cool features from Java. I have no patience for anyone who insists that I embrace the One True Programming Language; instead, I believe that salvation ought to be available to believers of any development creed.

COM helped us develop applications by assembling purchased components; we didn't have to write everything from scratch.

With the release of COM in 1993, Microsoft Windows developers found that they didn't have to write all of their application's code from scratch. COM allowed a client to call functions on a server at a binary level, without needing to compile source code. Using COM meant that we could buy components—say, a calendar control—from third-party vendors and wire them into our apps by writing a relatively thin layer of "glue" code to express our business logic. We got faster application development and better functionality than we could have written ourselves, and the third-parties got a much higher unit volume over which to amortize their development efforts. Microsoft also used COM to provide access to operating system functionality, such as queuing and transactions, again making apps faster and easier to write. It was a good idea, and the software gods smiled. For a while.

COM only went so far. We need to abstract away the differences in implementations.

As with most software architectures, COM helped to a certain point, but its internal structure has now become an obstacle rather than a help. COM has two main problems: First, it requires a substantial infrastructure from each application; for example, class factories and interface marshalers. Every development environment has to supply its own implementation of these mechanisms, so they're all slightly different and not as compatible as we'd like. Second, COM operates by keeping client and server at arm's length. They deal with each other through external interfaces, not through sharing their internal implementations. You might say that a COM client and server only make love by telephone. Unfortunately, everyone's implementation of a COM interface differs in sneaky and hard-to-reconcile ways. For example, strings are implemented differently in C++ than they are in Microsoft Visual Basic, and both are implemented differently than strings in Java. Passing a string from a COM server written in Visual Basic to a COM client written in C++ requires work on someone's part to iron out the differences, usually the C++ application because Visual Basic's implementation isn't negotiable. Programmers spend an inordinate amount of time ironing out these differences. That wastes valuable programmer time (and annoys programmers, making them change jobs to do something more fun), and you never know when you have it right, when any COM client regardless of implementation can use your server. We need to iron out differences in implementation, allowing our apps to interoperate on a more intimate basis.

The Web is nothing if not heterogeneous. That's the dominant feature that any successful software architecture has to deal with. Much as Microsoft would like to see Windows PCs everywhere, they're starting to realize that it isn't going to happen. We'd like to be able to write software once and run it on a variety of platforms. That's what Java promised but hasn't quite delivered. (Spare me the righteous e-mails disagreeing with that statement; this is MY book.) Even if we can't make that approach work completely today, we'd like our software architecture to allow platform interoperability to evolve in the future.

We'd like our code to be able to run on a variety of platforms.

One of the major causes of program failure today, particularly in applications that run for a long time, is memory leaks. A programmer allocates a block of memory from the operating system, intending to free it later, but forgets and allocates another block. The first block of memory is said to be "leaked away," as it can't be recovered for later use. If your app runs long enough, these

We need automatic memory management to prevent leaks.

leaks accumulate and the app runs out of memory. That's not a big deal in programs like Notepad that a user runs for a few minutes and then shuts down, but it's fatal in apps like Web servers that are supposed to run continuously for days or weeks. You'd think we could remember to free all of our memory allocations, but they often get lost in complex program logic. Like an automatic seat belt that passengers couldn't forget to buckle, we'd like a mechanism that would prevent memory leaks in some way that we couldn't forget to use.

We need help with managing different versions of the same software package.

When you ship a product, it's never perfect. (I know, yours are, but you'll have to agree that no one else's are, right? Besides, with no updates, how would you get more money from your existing customers?) So some time after you ship the first version, you ship an updated version of the product with new features and bug fixes for the old ones. Now the fun starts. No matter how hard you try to make your new release backward compatible with all of its old clients, this is very hard to do and essentially impossible to prove. We'd really like some standardized mechanism whereby servers can publish the version level they contain. We'd like this mechanism to enable clients to read the version level of available servers and pick one with which they are compatible or identify exactly what they are missing if they can't.

We'd like object-oriented programming features to be available in and between all programming languages.

Object-oriented programming, using such techniques as classes and inheritance, has permeated the software development world. That's about the only way you can manage programming efforts above a certain, not-very-high level of complexity. Unfortunately, every programming language provides a different combination of these features, naturally all incompatible, which means that different languages can interoperate with each other only at a very low level of abstraction. For example, COM does not allow a Visual Basic programmer to use the convenient mechanism of inheritance to extend an object written in C++. Instead, COM requires cumbersome workarounds. We'd like object-oriented programming techniques to be available in and between all programming languages.

The Web is fast becoming the main avenue by which users acquire software, which leads to major security problems. While current versions of Windows use digital certificates to identify the author of a piece of downloaded code, there is currently no way to ensure that a piece of code can't harm our systems, say, by scrambling files. We can choose to install or not install a downloaded component on our system, but there is no good way to restrict its activities once it's there. It's an all-or-nothing decision, and we really don't like that. We'd like some way of setting allowed and forbidden operations for various pieces of code and of having the operating system enforce those restrictions. For example, we might like to say that a piece of code we've just downloaded can read files but can't write them.

For safety, we want to be able to restrict the operations of pieces of code we don't fully trust.

The Windows operating system has grown almost unimaginably complex. From its humble beginnings as a Solitaire host with just a couple of hundred functions, it's mushroomed into a behemoth FreeCell host with over 5000 separate functions. You can't find the one you want simply by looking at an alphabetical list; it takes too long. Programmers manage complex projects by organizing their software into logical objects. We need a similar method of organizing the functionality of the operating system into logically related groups so that we have at least some chance of finding the function we want.

We need a better way of organizing operating system functions for better access.

Finally, I don't want to dump on COM too badly. It was revolutionary in its day, and we're going to have a lot of it with us for the foreseeable future. Just as the first color TV sets needed to also receive the black and white broadcasts that predominated at the time, so does whatever object model we start using need to seamlessly interoperate with COM, both as client and as server.

Our new object model needs to seamlessly interoperate with COM, both as client and as server.

It should be obvious that this long list of requirements is far more than any application vendor can afford to develop on its own. We have reached the limit of our potentialities. To move into the Internet world, we need a higher power that can provide us with a world we can live in.

Solution Architecture

The solution is managed code, executing in the Common Language Runtime.

The .NET Framework is Microsoft's operating system product that provides prefabricated solutions to these programming problems. The key to the framework is *managed code*. Managed code runs in an environment, called the *Common Language Runtime* (CLR), that provides a richer set of services than the standard Win32 operating system, as shown in Figure 2-1. The CLR environment is the higher power that we have to turn our code over to in order to deal with the harsh, savage world that is modern Internet programming.

Figure 2-1 *Managed execution in the Common Language Runtime.*

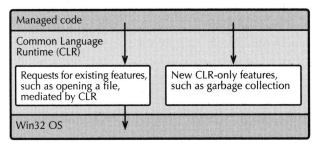

But with that architecture, how can the CLR work with any language? Not to sound Clintonesque, but that depends on what your definition of "language" is. Every CLR-compliant development tool compiles its own source code into a standard *Microsoft Intermediate Language* (MSIL, or IL for short), as shown in Figure 2-2. Because all development tools produce the same IL, regardless of the language in which their source code is written, differences in implementation are gone by the time they reach the CLR. No matter how it's presented in the source code programming language itself, every program's internal implementation of a string is the same as every other program's because they all use the *String* object within the CLR. The same holds true for arrays and classes and everything else.

Figure 2-2   *Different source code programming languages are compiled into MSIL.*

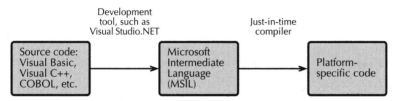

Any company that wants to can write a CLR-compliant language. Microsoft Visual Studio.NET provides CLR-compliant versions of Visual Basic, C# (pronounced C sharp), JScript, and C++. Third parties are producing many others, including APL, COBOL, and Perl.

All CLR-compliant source code languages compile to the same intermediate language.

The IL code produced by the development tool can't run directly on any computer. A second step is required, called *just-in-time* (JIT) compilation, as shown in Figure 2-2. A tool called a *just-in-time compiler*, or JITter, reads the IL and produces actual machine code that runs on that platform. This provides .NET with a certain amount of platform independence, as each platform can have its own JITter. Microsoft isn't making a huge deal about just-in-time compiling, as Sun did about Java 5 years or so ago, because this feature is still in its infancy. No CLR implementations for platforms other than Windows 2000 have currently been announced, although I expect some will be over time. It's probably more a strategy for covering future versions of Windows, like the forthcoming 64-bit version and now Windows XP, than it is for covering different operating systems, like Linux.

The IL is compiled just-in-time to run on the target machine.

The .NET Framework provides automatic memory management via garbage collection.

The .NET Framework provides automatic memory management, using a mechanism called *garbage collection*. A program does not have to explicitly free memory that it has allocated. The CLR detects when the program is no longer using the memory and automatically recycles it. Wish I had a maid that did that with my laundry!

The .NET Framework supports explicit standardized version management.

The .NET Framework finally supports versioning. Microsoft .NET provides a standardized way in which developers of servers can specify the version that resides in a particular EXE or DLL and a standardized mechanism that a client uses to specify which version it needs to run with. The operating system will enforce the version requests of clients, both providing a default set of versioning behavior and allowing a developer to override it and specify explicit versioning behavior.

The .NET Framework extends rich object-oriented programming features to all languages.

Because each language compiles to the same IL, all languages that support the CLR have the potential to support the same set of features. While it is possible to write a CLR language that does not expose this or that underlying CLR feature to a programmer, I expect the brutal Darwinian jungle that is the modern software marketplace to kill off such an ill-conceived idea very quickly. The CLR provides a rich set of object-oriented programming features, such as inheritance and parameterized object construction. Don't worry if these sound like complicated concepts—they aren't hard to use; they save you a lot of time and potential errors; and you'll grow to like both of them.

The .NET Framework organizes system functionality into a hierarchical namespace.

The .NET Framework organizes operating system functionality through the System namespace. All operating system objects, interfaces, and functions are now organized in a hierarchical manner, so it's much easier to find the things you want. It also keeps your object and function names from colliding with those of the operating system and those of other developers.

The .NET Framework supports code access security. You can specify that a piece of code is allowed to perform this operation but not that one. For example, you can allow a piece of code to read files but not write them, and the CLR will enforce your specifications and block any attempt to go outside them. This means that you can apply different levels of trust to code from different sources, just as you apply different levels of trust to different people that you deal with. This capability lets you run code from the Web without worrying that it's going to trash your system.

The .NET Framework supports code security.

Finally, the .NET Framework provides seamless interoperability with COM, both as client and as server. The framework puts a wrapper object around a COM object that makes the object look like a native .NET object. This means .NET code doesn't know or greatly care which kind of object it's running with. On the flip side, .NET objects know how to register themselves with an abstraction layer so that they appear to COM clients to be COM servers.

The .NET Framework provides seamless interoperability with COM, both as client and as server.

Oh Yeah? What Does It Cost?

But what about Platt's Second Law? (The amount of crap in the universe is conserved; see Chapter 1.) If I have less crap to deal with—for example, if I no longer have to worry about freeing memory that I've allocated—whose head did that crap get dumped on because it didn't just disappear. In the case of .NET, it got dumped primarily on two sets of heads, namely Microsoft's and Intel's. (All of my readers who work for Sun just stood up and cheered. Both of them.) In Microsoft's case, the operating system itself got harder to write. An automatic garbage collection mechanism like the one in .NET is several orders of magnitude harder to write than a simple in-out heap manager of the type that Windows 2000 contains. Since Microsoft hopes to sell millions of copies of .NET, they can afford to hire lots of smart programmers and engineer the heck out of it. This division of labor—letting Microsoft develop infrastructure while you worry less—makes economic sense.

The operating system got harder to write, but you don't really care about that.

In the case of Intel, the new .NET Framework will keep them busy producing faster CPUs and more memory chips. Some Microsoft marketingbozos (that's a single word that I've just coined) will claim that .NET apps are just as fast as non .NET apps, but they simply aren't and never will be. Sophisticated garbage collection requires more computation than simple heap allocation, just as an automatic seatbelt requires more parts than a manual one. Plus, since garbage collection doesn't take place as often, your computer probably needs more memory so that your app still has enough while objects are hanging around waiting to be garbage collected. (Remember Grosch's Law? Go check the end of Chapter 1 if you don't.) But I don't think that the additional memory and CPU cycles a .NET program requires are being squandered, as they are on that stupid dancing paper clip in Office. I think they're being wisely invested, saving you time and money by letting you write code faster and with fewer bugs because the operating system is doing more of the scut work for you. An application using a general disk operating system will never run as fast as one that programs absolute sector and track disk head movements. But you can't afford to do that; it takes too long, it costs too much, and you can't manage very much data. You'll spend all your time on the silly disk sectors and never get any paying work done. Once it becomes possible to abstract away these infrastructural problems, it becomes necessary to do it. If your own memory management was working well enough, you wouldn't be spending your debugging time tracking memory leaks.

Simplest Example

As I'll do throughout this book, I've written the simplest example I could think of to demonstrate the operation of the .NET Framework. You can download this sample and all the other code examples in this book from *www.introducingmicrosoft.net*. I wrote a .NET object server, the .NET replacement for an ActiveX DLL in Visual Basic 6, and its accompanying client. The server provides a single object exposing a single method, called *GetTime*, that provides the current system time in the form of a string, either with or without the seconds digits. Even though I wrote the server in Visual Basic and the client in C#, I didn't have to use Visual Studio. In fact, I wrote both applications in Notepad and built them with the command line tools provided in the .NET SDK. I do show examples of using Visual Studio.NET in other sections of this chapter. Note: You can download a copy of the .NET SDK at *www.msdn.microsoft.com/net*.

Figure 2-3 shows the code listing for my sample object server. It seems, at least superficially, quite similar to the classic Visual Basic code you are already familiar with. However, Microsoft made a number of important changes to the .NET version of Visual Basic to enable it to use .NET's CLR classes and interoperate correctly with the other CLR languages. A full discussion of these changes is far beyond the scope of this book, but as an example, arrays now begin with element(0) instead of element(1). If you declare an array with ten members (*Dim x(10) As Integer*), the members are numbered 0-9 instead of 1-10 as you are used to. The C++ guys and the VB guys arm-wrestled to see whose array syntax would be used consistently throughout the CLR, and the C++ guys won. Sorry. Sort of. These changes mean that you cannot simply compile your existing VB code in Visual Studio.NET and expect it to work correctly. It will take some effort; not an enormous amount, but more than the zero-level you were hoping for. (For some late-breaking news, see the note at the end of this chapter.)

Visual Basic.NET contains a number of critical language differences from Visual Basic 6.

Note

Visual Studio.NET contains an upgrade tool that runs automatically when you open a Visual Basic 6 project. It flags the changes that it detects and suggests fixes. The language has definitely gotten more powerful. If you want the cool Internet features of .NET, you'll probably think it's worth the effort to switch. Even if you're just writing single-user desktop form applications, you may still find the versioning support and the easier deployment and cleanup to be worth it.

Looking at our object server code, we first see the *Imports* directive. This new feature of Visual Basic.NET tells the compiler to "import the namespaces." The term *namespace* is a fancy way to refer to the description of a set of prefabricated functionality provided by some class somewhere. It is conceptually identical to a reference in your Visual Basic 6 project. The names following *Imports* tell the engine which sets of functionality to include the references for. In this case, *Microsoft.VisualBasic* is the one containing the definition of the *Now* function that I use to fetch the time. If you use Visual Basic from within Visual Studio.NET, the Visual Basic namespace is imported automatically without needing an explicit statement.

We next see the directive *Namespace TimeComponentNS*. This is the declaration of my component's namespace; the name that my clients will use when they want to access my component's functionality. I discuss namespaces later in this chapter. Again, if you are using Visual Studio.NET, this declaration is made automatically.

Figure 2-3 *Visual Basic code listing of simplest object server.*

```vb
' Import the external Visual Basic namespace, allowing me to
' access the Now function by its short name.

Imports Microsoft.VisualBasic

' Declare the namespace that clients will use to access
' the classes in this component.

Namespace TimeComponentNS

' Declare the class(es) that this DLL will provide to a client.
' This is the same as VB6.

Public Class TimeComponent

    ' Declare the function(s) that this class will provide to a client.
    ' This, too, is the same as VB6.

    Public Function GetTime(ByVal ShowSeconds As Boolean) As String

        ' The formatting of dates, and the returning of values of
        ' functions, changed somewhat in Visual Basic.NET.

        If (ShowSeconds = True) Then
            Return Now.ToLongTimeString
        Else
            Return Now.ToShortTimeString
        End If

    End Function

End Class

End Namespace
```

Next come the class and function declarations, identical to Visual Basic 6. Finally, I put in the internal logic of fetching the time, formatting it into a string and returning it to the client. These too

This section describes the code of my .NET object server.

have changed slightly. The property *Now* still fetches the date, but formatting it into a string is now done with a method of the new .NET class *DateTime* rather than a separate function. Also, a Visual Basic function specifies its return value using the new keyword *Return* instead of the syntax used in earlier versions.

Compiling the Visual Basic code produces a DLL containing intermediate language and metadata.

I next compiled my code into a DLL, named timecomponent.dll, using the command line tools that come with the .NET SDK. Anyone who cares to can find the command line syntax in the sample code you downloaded from the book's web site. The result may look like a plain old DLL to you, but it's actually very different inside. The Visual Basic.NET compiler didn't convert the Visual Basic code to native code; that is, to specific instructions for the microprocessor chip inside your PC. Instead, the DLL contains my object server's logic expressed in MSIL (again, for Microsoft Intermediate Language; IL for short), the intermediate language that I introduced in the "Solution Architecture" section in this chapter. All CLR language compilers produce this IL rather than native processor instructions, which is how the CLR can run seamlessly with so many different ones. The DLL also contains *metadata* that describes the code to the CLR system. This metadata is in a CLR-required format that describes the contents of the DLL: what classes and methods it contains, what external objects it requires, what version of the code it represents, and so on. Think of it as a type library on steroids. The main difference is that a COM server could sometimes run without a type library, whereas a .NET object server can't even begin to think about running without its metadata. I discuss this metadata further in the section, "Assemblies," later in the chapter.

Having written my server, I next need a client to test it. To demonstrate the fact that .NET works between different languages, I wrote this client in C#. I know that not many of you are familiar with this language; nobody is at this point. But if you look at the code in Figure 2-4, you'll see that it's fairly easy to understand at this level of simplicity. In fact, given the enhancements to Visual Basic.NET to support the CLR's object-oriented features such as inheritance (described later in this chapter), I've heard programmers after a few beers describe C# as "VB with semicolons" or occasionally "Java without Sun." Either one of these can start a fistfight if you say it too loudly in the wrong bar in Redmond or Sunnyvale.

Visual Basic and C# resemble each other more than either community likes to admit.

Figure 2-4 *C# code listing of simplest object client.*

```
// Import the namespaces that this program uses, thereby allowing
// us to use the short names of the functions inside them.

using System ;
using TimeComponentNS ;

class MainApp
{
    // The static method "Main" is an application's entry point.

    public static void Main()
    {
        // Declare and create a new component of the class
        // provided by the VB server we wrote.

        TimeComponent tc = new TimeComponent ( ) ;

        // Call the server's GetTime method. Write its
        // resulting string to a console window.

        Console.Write (tc.GetTime (true)) ;
    }
}
```

Our client example starts with importing namespaces, which in C# requires the directive *using*. Our sample client imports the System namespace (described in detail later in this chapter), which contains the description of the *Console.Write* function and our time component's namespace. We have to explicitly tell the compiler in which DLL it will find our namespace. We do this in the compiler batch file. Visual Studio.NET provides an easy user interface for this.

Execution of any C# program begins in a static method called *Main*. In that method, we can see that our client program uses the C# *new* operator to tell the CLR engine to find the DLL containing our *TimeComponent* class and create an instance of it. The next line calls the object's *GetTime* method and then uses the system's *Console.Write* method to output the time string in a command line window. The C# compiler in this case produces an EXE file. Like the server DLL, this EXE does not contain native instructions, but instead contains intermediate language and metadata.

The C# client also compiles to intermediate language.

When I run the C# client executable, the system loader notes that it is managed code and loads it into the CLR engine. The engine will note that the EXE contains IL, so it will invoke the just-in-time compiler, or JITter. The JITter is a system tool that converts IL into native code for whichever processor and operating system it runs on. Each different architecture will have its own JITter tailored to that particular system, thereby allowing one set of IL code to run on multiple types of systems. The JITter produces native code, which the CLR engine will begin to execute. When the client invokes the *new* operator to create an object of the *TimeComponent* class, the CLR engine will again invoke the JITter to compile the component DLL's IL just-in-time and then make the call and report the results. The output is shown in Figure 2-5.

Figure 2-5 *Console output of sample TimeClient program.*

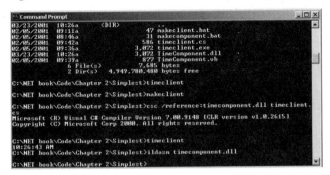

This run-time compilation model works well for some classes of applications, such as code downloaded from the Internet for a page you just surfed to, but not for others, say, Visual Studio, which you use all day, every day, and update once or twice a year. Therefore, an application can specify that JIT compilation is to be performed once, when the application is installed on a machine, and the native code stored on the system as it is for non-.NET applications. You do this via the command-line utility program Ngen.exe, the native image generator, not shown in this example.

The IL is compiled just-in-time when the client and its component are run.

When the client used the *new* operator to create the object, how did the loader know where to find the server DLL? In this case, the loader simply looked in the same directory as the client application. This is known as a *private assembly*, the simplest type of deployment model in .NET. A private assembly can't be referenced from outside its own directory. It supports no version checking or any security checking. It requires no registry entries, as a COM server would. To uninstall a private assembly, all you have to do is delete the files, without performing any other cleanup. Obviously, this simple case, while effective in situations like this, isn't useful in every situation—for example, when you want to share the same

The loader finds the DLL requested by the client by looking in the client application's directory.

server code among multiple clients. I discuss these more complex scenarios in the section on assemblies later in this chapter.

More on .NET Namespaces

I remember programming Windows version 2.0, scanning the alphabetical list of operating system functions (on paper, that's how long ago this was) until I found the one whose name seemed to promise that it would do what I wanted. I'd try it, and sometimes it would work and sometimes it wouldn't. If it didn't, I'd go back to scanning the list again. Listing the functions alphabetically worked reasonably well on Windows 2.0, which contained only a few hundred different functions. I could see at a glance (or two or three) everything that the operating system could do for me, which gave me a fighting chance at writing some decent, albeit limited, code.

Selecting items from a short alphabetical list is easy.

It's much harder when the list gets longer.

Organizing operating system functions into one alphabetical list won't work with today's 32-bit Windows. It's enormous—over 5000 functions. I can't scan through a list that long to find, for example, console output functions; they're scattered among far too many unrelated functions for me to pick them out. It's a problem for operating system designers, too. When they want to add a new function, they have to choose a name for it that is descriptive but that doesn't conflict with all the other function names already implemented. Application programmers also need to make sure that their global function names don't conflict with operating system functions. The signal-to-noise ratio of this approach gets lower as the list of functions gets longer, and it's approaching absolute zero today. We say that the *namespace*, the set of names within which a particular name needs to be unique, has gotten too large.

The way to handle large lists is to break them down into smaller sublists that you can more easily digest. The classic example of this is the Start button menu in Windows. If every application on your entire computer were listed on one gigantic menu, you'd never be able to find the one that you wanted. Instead, the Start menu provides a relatively short (10 or so) list of groups, easy to scan and pick from. Each group contains a list of logical subgroups, nested as deeply as you feel is cost-effective, eventually terminating in a short list of actual applications. By the time you pick the application you want, you've looked at maybe 50 different choices, never more than a dozen or so at a time. Think how much easier this is compared to selecting the one application you want out of the thousand or so installed on most computers.

The .NET Framework provides a better way of organizing operating system functions and objects. This same mechanism keeps the names of functions and objects that you write from interfering with the names of objects and functions written by other developers. It uses the concept of a namespace, which is a logical subdivision of software functionality within which all names must be unique. It's not a new concept; object-oriented languages have used it for decades. But its use in .NET is the first time I know of that an entire operating system's functionality has been organized in this way.

All .NET CLR objects and functions are part of a namespace called System. When you look them up in the documentation, you'll find that all names begin with the characters "System." We say that all the objects and functions whose names begin this way "belong to the System namespace." The System namespace is naturally quite large, as it contains the names of all functional elements of a rich

> The best way to handle large lists is to break them down into smaller logical groups.

> .NET provides the concept of a namespace, a logical division within which a name needs to be unique.

> All .NET CLR objects and functions live within the System namespace.

operating system. It is therefore subdivided into a number of subordinate namespaces—for example, System.Console, which contains all the functions dealing with input and output on a console window. Some of these subnamespaces contain their own subsubnamespaces, and so on down the line until the developers got tired of it. The *fully qualified name* of a function, sometimes called the *qualified name* or *q-name*, is the name of the function preceded by its full namespace location, also known as a *qualifier*. For example, *System.Console.Write* is the fully qualified name of the system function that writes output to a console window. You can call a function by means of its fully qualified name from anywhere in your code.

The *System* namespace is implemented in several separate DLLs, so you have to make sure that your development tools know to include all the ones you need.

The System namespace is very large. Consequently, it is implemented in several separate DLLs. Just because a function or an object is part of the System namespace does not necessarily mean that your editor, compiler, and linker will automatically be able to find it. You generally have to tell your development tools which of the System namespace DLLs you want to include when building a project. For example, I often build .NET components in Visual Studio, and I often like to pop up message boxes from those components during debugging. The *MessageBox* object is part of the System.Windows.Forms namespace, which is implemented in System.Windows.Forms.dll. Visual Studio does not automatically include this DLL in its reference list when you create a component library project, probably because its authors figured that components would work behind the scenes and not interact with the user. I have to explicitly add that reference to my project if I want access to the *MessageBox* object.

This organization of functions into logical groups is very handy for finding the one you want with a minimum of fuss. The only drawback is that fully qualified names can get very long. For example, the function *System.Runtime.InteropServices.Marshal.*

ReleaseComObject is used for releasing a specified COM object immediately without performing a full garbage collection. (See the section ".NET Memory Management" for an explanation of the latter.) Most .NET applications won't use this function at all, but the ones that do will probably use it in many places. Typing this whole thing in every time you call it could get very tedious very quickly. My wife does not address me as "David Samuel Platt, son of Benjamin, son of Joseph" unless she is exceptionally angry, a state she is incapable of occupying for very long. Therefore, just as people address their most intimate relations by their first names, the CLR allows you to *import a namespace*, as shown earlier in the programming examples in Figures 2-3 and 2-4. When you import a namespace, you're telling your compiler that you use the functions in that namespace so often that you want to be on a first-name basis with them. Importing a namespace is done in Visual Basic by using the keyword *Imports*, and in C# via the keyword *using*. For example, in Figure 2-4, I imported the namespace *System*, which allowed me to write to the console by calling *Console.Write*. If I hadn't imported the *System* namespace, I would have had to use the fully qualified name *System.Console.Write*. Conversely, I could have imported *System.Console*, and simply called *Write*. Choosing which namespaces to import is entirely a matter of your own convenience and has no effect on the final product other than allowing you to organize your own thought processes so as to produce your best output. Since the whole point of using separate namespaces is to separate functions with the same name to prevent conflicts, you can't import them all at the same time. To avoid confusion, I strongly urge you to pick a consistent set of rules for choosing which namespaces to import and follow it throughout your entire project.

Importing a namespace allows you to use short names when calling a function within that namespace.

When you write a .NET object server, you specify the name of the namespace in which your code lives. This is done via the *Namespace* directive, as shown in Figure 2-3. The namespace will

Your own code will also live in a namespace, with a name you select.

often be the same as the name of the file in which the code lives, but it doesn't have to be. You can have more than one namespace in the same file, or you can spread one namespace among multiple files. Visual Studio.NET or other development environments will often automatically assign a namespace to your project. But how do you know that your namespace won't conflict with the namespace chosen by another vendor for a different component? That's what assemblies are for, which is our next topic of conversation.

Assemblies

.NET makes extensive use of a new packaging unit called an assembly.

The .NET Framework makes extensive use of *assemblies* for .NET code, resources, and metadata. All code that the .NET runtime executes must reside in an assembly. In addition, all security, namespace resolution, and versioning features work on a per-assembly basis. Since assemblies are used so often and for so many different things, I need to discuss assemblies in some detail.

Concept of an Assembly

An assembly is a logical collection of one or more EXE or DLL files containing an application's code and resources. An assembly also contains a *manifest*, which is a metadata description of the code and resources "inside" the assembly. (I'll explain those quotes in a second.) An assembly can be, and often is, a single file, either an EXE or a DLL, as shown in Figure 2-6.

Our simple example produced two single-file assemblies

When we built the simple example of a time server earlier in this chapter, the DLL that our compiler produced was actually an assembly. The EXE client application that we built in that example was another single-file assembly. When you use tools such as Visual Studio.NET, each project will most likely correspond to a single assembly.

Figure 2-6 *Single-file and multifile assemblies.*

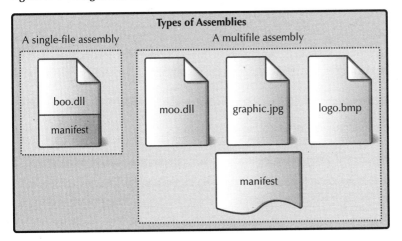

Although an assembly often resides in a single file, it also can be, and often is, a logical, not a physical, collection of more than one file residing in the same directory, as shown in Figure 2-6. The manifest specifying the files that comprise the assembly can reside in one of the code-containing EXEs or DLLs of the assembly, or it can live in a separate EXE or DLL that contains nothing but the manifest. When dealing with a multifile assembly, you *must* remember that the files are not tied together by the file system in any way. It is entirely up to you to ensure that the files called out in the manifest are actually present when the loader comes looking for them. The only thing that makes them part of the assembly is that they are mentioned in the manifest. In this case, the term *assembly*, with its connotation of metal parts bolted together, is not the best term. Perhaps "roster" might be a better one. That's why I put quotes around the term "inside" the assembly a few paragraphs ago. You add and remove files from a multifile assembly using the command line SDK utility program AL.exe, the Assembly Generation Utility. Smart development environments such as Visual Studio do this automatically for you.

An assembly can also be a logical collection of more than one file.

You can view an
assembly's manifest
with ILDASM.exe

You can view the manifest of an assembly using the IL Disassembler (ILDASM.exe). Figure 2-7 shows the manifest of our time component. You can see that it lists the external assemblies on which this assembly depends. In this case, we depend on mscorlib.dll, the main .NET CLR DLL, and on an assembly called Microsoft.Visual-Basic, which contains Visual Basic's internal functions such as *Now*. It also lists the assembly names that we provide to the world, in this case, TimeComponent.

Figure 2-7   *Assembly manifest of our sample time component.*

```
MANIFEST                                                          _ □ ×
.assembly extern mscorlib
{
  .publickeytoken = (B7 7A 5C 56 19 34 E0 89 )           // .z\V.4.
  .hash = (B0 73 F2 4C 14 39 0A 35 25 EA 45 0F 60 58 C3 84   // .s.L.9.5%.E.`X..
           E0 3B E0 95 )                                     // .;..
  .ver 1:0:2411:0
}
.assembly extern Microsoft.VisualBasic
{
  .publickeytoken = (B0 3F 5F 7F 11 D5 0A 3A )           // .?_....
  .hash = (A3 11 69 32 7F 24 F4 A4 0D EB 55 F9 31 63 78 BD   // ..i2.$....U.1cx.
           A8 BE 91 FB )
  .ver 7:0:9135:0
}
.assembly TimeComponent
{
  .hash algorithm 0x00008004
  .ver 0:0:0:0
}
.module TimeComponent.dll
// MVID: {20A87166-3129-4FD2-9B47-FF675C9F66E0}
.subsystem 0x00000002
.file alignment 512
.corflags 0x00000001
// Image base: 0x03060000
```

In addition to the code objects exposed by and required by the assembly, the manifest also contains information that describes the assembly itself. For example, it contains the assembly's version information, expressed in a standardized format described later in this section. It can also describe the culture (fancy name for human language and sublanguage, say, Australian English) for which the assembly is written. In the case of a shared assembly, of which more anon, the manifest contains a public cryptographic key, which is used to ensure that the assembly can be distinguished from all other assemblies regardless of its filename. You can even add your own custom attributes to the manifest, which the CLR will ignore. You set manifest attributes with the Assembly Generation Utility mentioned previously or with Visual Studio.NET.

Assemblies and Deployment

The central question in dividing your code among assemblies is whether the code inside the assembly is intended solely for your own application's use or will be shared with any other application that wants it. Microsoft.NET supports both options, but it requires more footwork in the latter case. In the case of code that you write for your own applications, say, the calculation engine for a complex financial instrument, you'd probably want to make the assembly private. On the other hand, a general utility object that could reasonably be used by many applications—a file compression engine, for example—might be better used if you make it shared.

You need to think carefully about whether your assemblies should be private or public.

Suppose you want your assemblies to be private. The .NET model couldn't be simpler. In fact, that's exactly what I did in the simplest example shown previously. You just build a simple DLL assembly, and copy it to the directory of the client assembly that uses it or to a subdirectory of that client. You don't have to make any entries in the system registry or Active Directory as you had to do when using COM components. None of the code will change unless you change it, so you will never encounter the all-too-familiar situation in which a shared DLL changes versions up or down and your app breaks for no apparent reason.

Assemblies can be private to an application, which simplifies your life in certain cases.

The obvious problem with this approach is the proliferation of assemblies, which was the problem DLLs were originally created to solve back in Windows 1.0. If every application that uses, say, a text box, needs its own copy of the DLL containing it, you'll have assemblies breeding like bacteria all over your computer. Jeffrey Richter argues (in *MSDN Magazine*, March 2001) that this isn't a

However, sometimes you want the code in assemblies to be shared.

problem. With 40 gigabyte hard drives selling today for under $200, everyone can afford all the disk space they need, so most assemblies should be private; that way your application will never break from someone else messing with shared code. That's like an emergency room doctor saying that the world would be a far better place if people didn't drink to excess or take illegal drugs. They're both absolutely right, but neither's vision is going to happen any time soon in the real world. Richter's idea is practical for developers, who usually get big, fast PCs, but a customer with a large installed base of two-year-old PCs that it can't junk or justify upgrading at that point in its budget cycle isn't going to buy that argument *or* bigger disks. Fairly soon in your development process, you will need to share an assembly among several applications, and you want the .NET Framework to help you do that.

The .NET Framework allows you to share assemblies by placing them in the *global assembly cache* (GAC, pronounced like the cartoon exclamation). This is a directory on your machine, currently \\winnt\assembly, in which all shared assemblies are required to live. You can place assemblies into the cache, view their properties, and remove them from the cache using a .NET SDK command line utility called GACUTIL.exe, which works well when run from scripts and batch files. Most human users will prefer to use the Assembly Cache Viewer, which is a shell extension that installs with the .NET SDK. It automatically snaps into Windows Explorer and provides you with the view of the GAC shown in Figure 2-8.

Whenever you share any type of computer file, you run up against the problem of name collisions. Because all .NET shared assemblies have to go in the GAC so that they can be managed, we need some way of definitively providing unique names for all the code files that live there, even if their original names were the same. This is done with a *strong name*, otherwise know as a *shared name*. A strong name uses public key cryptography to transparently produce a name that is guaranteed to be unique among all assemblies in the system. The manifest of a shared assembly contains the public key of a public/private key pair. The combination of the file's name and an excerpt from this public key is the strong name.

Figure 2-8 *Global Assembly Cache Viewer.*

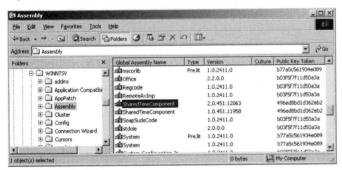

Suppose we want to write a shared assembly that lives in the GAC. I've switched to Visual Studio.NET for this example, both to demonstrate it and because I find it easier to operate than the command line tools. I've written a different Visual Basic.NET component that does the same thing as our simplest time example, except that it adds the characters "Shared example:" to its returned time string so that you can differentiate it from the first example. Once I build the component, I need to generate and assign a strong name for it, also known as *signing* the component. Visual Studio.NET can be configured to do this automatically, as shown in Figure 2-9, if you provide a file containing the public/private key pair. You generate this with the SDK command line utility program SN.exe. When I build the component, Visual Studio.NET signs it automatically. I then manually put it in the GAC by using Windows Explorer.

Figure 2-9 *Visual Studio generating a strong name.*

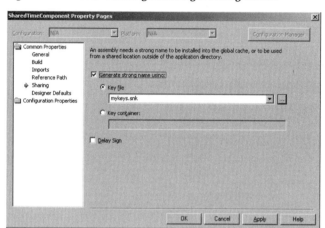

This paragraph contains instructions for generating a shared assembly.

I've also provided a client, this one written in Visual Basic using Visual Studio.NET, that uses the shared assembly. I tell Visual Studio.NET to generate a reference to the server DLL by right-clicking on the References folder in the Solution Explorer window (shown in Figure 2-10), selecting Add Reference, and then clicking Browse and surfing over to the shared assembly file that resides in a standard directory.

Visual Studio cannot currently add a reference to an assembly in the GAC, although this feature is promised for a future release. This happened because the GAC's design hadn't yet stabilized by the time the Visual Studio developers needed to design their reference mechanism. Therefore, unless they're building client and server together as part of the same project, developers must install two copies of their components, one in a standard directory to compile against and another in the GAC for their clients to run against. Users will require only the latter. Visual Studio.NET generates a reference class accessing that namespace.

I then need to set the *CopyLocal* property of that reference to False, thereby telling Visual Studio.NET that I don't want it to make a local copy. When the client runs, the loader looks for a local copy, doesn't find it, and therefore checks the GAC.

Figure 2-10 *Adding a reference to a shared component.*

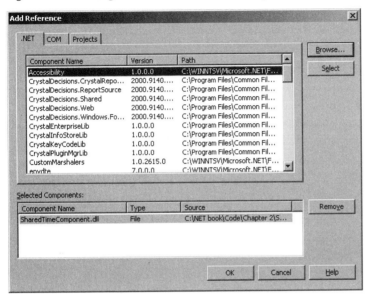

As an added benefit of the public key cryptography scheme used for signing shared assemblies, we also gain a check on the integrity of the assembly file. The assembly generator performs a hashing operation on the contents of the files contained in the manifest. It then encrypts the result of this hash using our private key and stores the encrypted result in the manifest. When the loader fetches an assembly from the GAC, it performs the same hashing algorithm on the assembly's file or files, decrypts the manifest's stored hash using the public key, and compares the two. If they match, the loader knows that the assembly's files haven't been tampered with. This doesn't get you any real identity checking because you can't be sure whose public key it really is, but it does guarantee that the assembly hasn't been tampered with since it was signed.

This paragraph contains instructions for writing a client that uses an object from the GAC.

The public/private key algorithm also provides a check on the integrity of the assembly's files.

Assemblies and Versioning

Versioning of code is an enormous, painful, unsexy problem.

Dealing with changes to published code has historically been an enormous problem, often known as DLL Hell. Replacing a DLL used by an existing client with a newer version bit you two ways, coming and going. First, the new code sometimes broke existing applications that depended on the original version. As hard as you try to make new code backward compatible with the old, you can never know or test everything that anyone was ever doing with it. It's especially annoying when you update a new DLL and don't run the now-broken old client until a month later, when it's very difficult to tell what you did that broke it. Second, updates come undone when installing an application copies an older DLL over a newer one that's already on your computer, thereby breaking an existing client that depended on the newer behavior. It happens all the time, when an installation script says, "Target file *xxx* exists and is newer than the source. Copy anyway?" and 90 percent of the time the user picks Yes. This one's especially maddening because someone else's application caused the problem, but your app's the one that won't work, your tech support line is the one that receives expensive calls and bomb threats, and you better hope you haven't sold any copies of the program to the Postal Service. Problems with versions cost an enormous amount of money in lost productivity and debugging time. Also, they keep people from buying upgrades or even trying them because they're afraid the upgrade will kill something else, and they're often right.

.NET finally incorporates some functionality for versioning.

Windows has so far ignored this versioning problem, forcing developers to deal with it piecemeal. There has never been, until .NET, any standardized way for a developer to specify desired versioning behavior and have the operating system enforce it. In .NET, Microsoft seems to have realized that this is a universal problem that can be solved only at an operating system level and has provided a system for managing different versions of code.

Every assembly contains version information in its manifest. This information consists of a *compatibility version*, which is a set of four numbers used by the CLR loader to enforce the versioning behavior requested by a client. The compatibility version number consists of a major and minor version number, a build number, and a revision number. The development tools that produce an assembly put the version information into the manifest. Visual Studio.NET stores its version numbers in attributes that you set in your project's AssemblyInfo.vb file, as shown in Figure 2-11. Command line tools require complex switches to specify an assembly's version. You can see the version number in the IL Disassembler at the bottom of Figure 2-12. You can also see it when you install the assembly in the GAC, as shown previously in Figure 2-8.

Figure 2-11 *AssemblyInfo.vb file showing version of component assembly.*

```
' Version information for an assembly consists of the following
' four values:
'
'       Major Version
'       Minor Version
'       Revision
'       Build Number
'
' You can specify all the values or you can default the Build and
' Revision Numbers by using the '*' as shown below:

<Assembly: AssemblyVersion("2.0.*")>
```

Figure 2-12 *ILDASM showing version of a server component.*

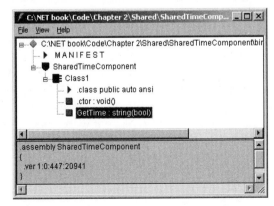

Each assembly contains information telling the runtime what version number it represents.

The manifest can also contain an *informational version*, which is a human readable string like "Microsoft .NET Beta 1 Sept 2000." The informational version is intended for display to human viewers and is ignored by the CLR.

Every client assembly contains information about the versions it was built against.

When you build a client assembly, you've seen that it contains the name of the external assemblies on which it depends. It also contains the version number of the external assembly that it was built against, as shown in Figure 2-13.

Figure 2-13 *ILDASM showing required version in a client.*

```
MANIFEST                                                    _ □ ×
}
.assembly extern SharedTimeComponent
{
  .publickeytoken = (49 6E D8 BD 1D 36 2E B2 )
  .hash = (A0 82 D1 EB BB 29 8F 64 FE EA 1B 42 F2 1F E5 11
           C1 58 DC 64 )
  .ver 1:0:449:10749
}
```

By default, a client requires the exact version of the server against which it was built.

When the client runs, the CLR looks to find the version that the client needs. The default versioning behavior requires the exact version against which the client was built; otherwise the load will fail. Since the GAC can contain different versions of the same assembly, as shown in Figure 2-8, you don't have the problem of a new version breaking old clients, or an older version mistakenly replacing a new one. You can keep all the versions that you need in the GAC, and each client assembly will request and receive the one that it has been written and tested against.

Occasionally this versioning behavior isn't what you want. You might discover a fatal side effect, perhaps a security hole, in the original version of the server, and need to replace it with a new one immediately. Or maybe you find a bug in the new server and have to roll the new clients back to use the old one. Rather than have to recompile all of your clients against the new version, as would be the case with a classic DLL, you can override the system's default behavior with a configuration file, as shown in Figure 2-14. The configuration file has the FULL name of the application that it configures, including the extension, with the additional extension ".config" tacked onto the end. The sample shown comes from the file named SharedTimeClient.exe.config. For each assembly, you can specify which newer version is to replace which older version.

You can override the system default with a configuration file.

Figure 2-14 *Versioning configuration file.*

```
<configuration>
    <runtime>
        <assemblyBinding xmlns="urn:schemas-microsoft-com:asm.v1">
            <dependentAssembly>
                <assemblyIdentity name="SharedTimeComponent"
                                  publicKeyToken="496ed8bd1d362eb2"/>
                <bindingRedirect oldVersion="1.0.451.11958"
                                 newVersion="2.0.451.19800" />
            </dependentAssembly>
        </assemblyBinding>
    </runtime>
</configuration>
```

Object-Oriented Programming Features

When a software project reaches a certain level of complexity, the sheer effort of organizing the source code, of remembering the internal workings of every function, overwhelms the effort of dealing with your problem domain. No single person can remember what all the functions do and how they fit together, and chaos results. This limitation isn't very large, perhaps a five-programmer project, arguably less. To develop larger and more functional pieces of software—Microsoft Word for example—we need a better way of organizing code than providing global functions all over the place. Otherwise, the effort of picking our way through our spaghetti code overwhelms the work of figuring out how to process words.

Organizing the internal functionality of software projects is difficult.

The techniques of object-oriented programming were developed to solve this problem and allow larger, more complex programs to be developed. Exactly what someone means when he uses the term "object-oriented" is hard to pin down. The meaning depends heavily on the term's usage context and the shared background of

The only way to successfully develop software projects larger than a few developers is to partition them into classes of objects.

the listeners. It's sort of like the word "love." I once watched, amused, as two respected authors argued vehemently for half an hour over whether a particular programming technique truly deserved the description "object-oriented" or only the lesser "object-based." But like love, most developers agree that object-oriented software is a Good Thing, even if they're somewhat vague on why and not completely sure about what. As most people will agree that the word "love," at the minimum, indicates that you like something a lot, so most programmers will agree that object-oriented programming involves at least the partitioning of a program into *classes*, which combine logically related sets of data with the functions that act on that data. An *object* is an individual instance of a class. *Cat* is a class, my pet Simba is an instance of the class, an object. If you do a good job of segregating your program's functionality into classes that make sense, your developers don't have to understand the functionality of the entire program. They can concentrate on the particular class or classes involved in their subset of it, with (hopefully) minimal impact from other classes.

Providing object-oriented functionality to a programmer has historically been the job of the programming language, and different languages have taken it to different levels. COBOL, for example, doesn't do it at all. Visual Basic provides a minimal degree of object-oriented functionality, essentially classes and nothing else. C++ and Java provide a high level of object-oriented features. Languages that want to work together seamlessly need to share the same degree of support for object-orientation, so the question facing Microsoft and developers was whether to smarten up Visual Basic and other non-object-oriented languages or dumb down C++ and other languages that did support object-orientation. Because the architects of .NET belong to the school of thought that says object-orientation is the only way to get anything useful done in the modern software industry, they decided that object-oriented features would be an integral part of the CLR environment, and thus available to all languages. The two most useful object-oriented techniques provided by the CLR are inheritance and constructors. I'll describe each of them in the following sections.

.NET provides all languages with the object-oriented features of inheritance and constructors.

Inheritance

Essentially no manufacturer in modern industry, with the possible exception of glass makers, builds their products entirely from nature, starting with earth, air, fire, and water. Instead, almost everyone reuses components that someone else has built, adding value in the process. For example, a company that sells camper trucks doesn't produce engine and chassis; instead they buy pickup trucks from an automaker and add specialized bodies to them. The auto maker in turn bought the windshields from a glass manufacturer, who bought sand from a digger. We would like our software development process to follow this model, starting with generic functionality that someone else has already written and adding our own specialized attachments to it.

Essentially all modern economic processes involve adding value to existing components.

The object-oriented programming technique known as inheritance makes development of components much easier for programmers of software objects than it is for makers of physical objects. Someone somewhere uses a programming language that supports inheritance to write an object class, called the *base class,* that provides some useful generic functionality, say, reading and writing bytes from a stream. We'd like to use this basic functionality, with our own twists in it, in a class that reads and writes like the base class but that also provides statistics such as length. So we write a piece of software, known as the *derived class,* that incorporates the base class's functionality but modifies it in some manner, either adding more pieces to it, replacing some portion of it while leaving the rest intact, or a combination of both. We do this by simply telling the compiler that our derived class inherits from the base class, using the syntax of our programming language. The compiler will automatically include the base class's functionality in our derived class by reference. Think of it as cutting and pasting without actually moving anything. The derived class is said to *inherit from, derive from,* or *extend* the base class. The process is shown in Figure 2-15 with several intervening classes omitted for clarity.

Object-oriented programming provides this concept in software by means of inheritance.

Figure 2-15 *Object-oriented programming inheritance.*

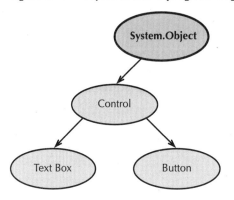

Every .NET object inherits from the system base class System.Object.

The .NET Framework uses inheritance to provide all kinds of system functionality, from the simplest string conversions to the most sophisticated Web Services. To explore inheritance further, let's start as always with the simplest example we can find. The time component I wrote previously in this chapter offers a good illustration of .NET's inheritance. Even though I didn't explicitly write code to say so, our time component class derives from the Microsoft-provided base class *System.Object*. You can see that this is so by examining the component with ILDASM, as shown in Figure 2-16. All objects in the .NET system, without exception, derive from *System.Object* or another class that in turn derives from it. If you don't specify a different base class, *System.Object* is implied. If you prefer a different base class, you specify it by using the keyword *Inherits* in Visual Basic, as shown in Figure 2-17, or the colon operator in C#.

Figure 2-16 *ILDASM showing inheritance from* **System.Object.**

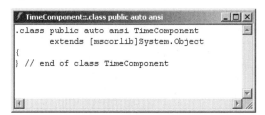

Figure 2-17 *Explicit declaration of inheritance.*

```
Namespace VS7DemoTimeService

    Public Class WebService1
        Inherits System.Web.Services.WebService
```

.NET provides much system functionality by means of inheritance.

In more complex cases, the Visual Studio.NET Object Browser shows us the inheritance tree. This case is too simple for it to handle. Figure 2-18 shows the Object Browser.

Figure 2-18 *The Visual Studio.NET Object Browser showing the inheritance tree.*

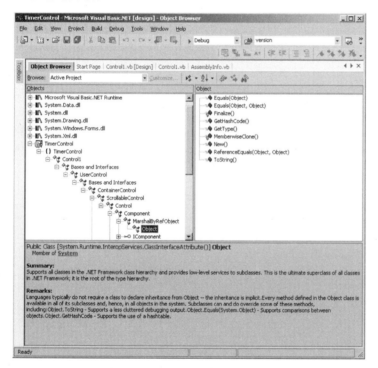

OK, our time component inherits functionality from *System.Object*, but how do we know what was in the will? We find that out with a little old-fashioned RTFM (Read The Funny Manual, more or less). When we do that, we find that our base class has the public methods shown in Table 2-1. That means that our derived class, the time component, knows how to do these things even though we didn't write code for them.

Table 2-1   Public methods of *System.Object*

Method name	Purpose
Equals	Determines whether this object is the same instance as a specified object.
GetHashCode	Quickly generates and returns an integer that can be used to identify this object in a hash table or other indexing scheme.
GetType	Returns the system metadata of the object
ToString	Returns a string that provides the object's view of itself.

The *Equals* method determines whether two object references do or do not refer to the same physical instance of an object. This determination was surprisingly difficult to make in COM and could easily be broken by an incorrectly implemented server, but in .NET our objects inherit this functionality free from the base class. I've written a client application that creates several instances of our time component and demonstrates the *Equals* method, among others. It's shown in Figure 2-19.

Figure 2-19   *Client program demonstrating* System.Object *features inherited by time component.*

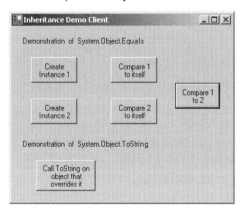

Sometimes your component doesn't want everything it inherits from a base class, just like human heirs. You love the antique table your Aunt Sophie left you, but you aren't real crazy about her flatulent bulldog (or vice versa). Software inheritance generally allows a derived class to *override* a method that it inherits from the base class: that is, provide a replacement for it. A good example of this is the method *System.Object.ToString*, which tells an object to return a string for display to a programmer who is debugging the application. The implementation that we inherit from *System.Object* simply returns the name of the derived class, which isn't that illuminating. To make our component easier to debug, we'd like this method to return more detailed information. For example, an object that represents an open file might return the name of that file. We do that by overriding the base class's method, as shown in Figure 2-20. We write a method in our derived class that has the same name and parameters as the method in the base class, specifying the keyword *Overrides* (*override* in C#) to tell the compiler to replace the base class's implementation with our derived class's new one.

You can override a base class's methods to replace part of its functionality.

Figure 2-20 *Overriding base class method.*

```
' This method overrides the ToString method of the
' universal base class System.Object.

Public Overrides Function ToString() As String

    ' Call the base class's ToString method and get the result.
    ' You don't have to do this if you don't want to. I did,
    ' for demo purposes.

    Dim BaseResult as String
    BaseResult = MyBase.ToString

    ' Construct response string with base class's string plus
    ' my own added information. The net result here is that
    ' I'm piggybacking on the base class, not completely
    ' replacing it.

    Return "You have reached the overriding class. " + _
           "The base class says: " + BaseResult

End Function
```

If your derived class wants to provide its own functionality in addition to that of the base class—rather than instead of the base class—it can call the overridden base class's method explicitly. In Visual Basic, the base class is accessible through the named object *MyBase*, and in C# it's called *base*. The sample component calls the base class to get its string and then appends its own string to that of the base class. The result is that the component is piggybacking on the base class's functionality rather than completely replacing it. Not all base class methods can be overridden. A base class method must be written with the keyword *Overridable* in VB or *virtual* in C# if you want to allow this.

An overriding method can access the base class's method that it overrides.

Much is made of .NET's ability to provide cross-language inheritance, that is, to allow a class written in one language, Visual Basic, for example, to derive from a base class written in another language, say C#. COM couldn't provide this feature because the differences between language implementations were too great. However, the standardized IL architecture of the CLR allows .NET applications to use it. In fact, the simple time component example does exactly that with no effort on my part. I guarantee you that the *System.Object* class is written in one language and not any other, yet every .NET object, without exception and regardless of language, inherits from it.

.NET inheritance works between different languages.

Object Constructors

As the Good Rats sang a couple of decades ago, "birth comes to us all." As humans mark births with various rituals (religious observances, starting a college fund), so objects need a location where their birth-ritual code can be placed. Object-oriented programming has long recognized the concept of a *class constructor*, a function called when an object is created. (Object-oriented programming also uses the concept of a *class destructor*, a function called when the object is destroyed, but this concept has been replaced in .NET with the system garbage collector described in

Objects need a standard place for putting initialization code.

the next section.) Different languages have implemented constructors differently—C++ with the class name, Visual Basic with *Class_Initialize*). As with so many features that have varied widely among languages, the rituals for object creation had to be standardized for code written in different languages to work together properly.

In .NET, Visual Basic lost its *Class_Initialize* event, and the model looks much more like a C++ model, primarily because parameterized constructors are needed to support inheritance. Every .NET class can have one or more constructor methods. This method has the name *New* in Visual Basic.NET or the class name in *C#*. The constructor function is called when a client creates your object using the *new* operator. In the function, you place the code that does whatever initialization your object requires, perhaps acquiring resources and setting them to their initial state. An example of a constructor is shown in Figure 2-21.

Figure 2-21 *Constructor example.*

.NET object classes provide this in the form of an object constructor.

```
Public Class ConstructorDemoComponent

    Dim m_x, m_y As Integer

    Public Overloads Sub New ( )

        MyBase.New ( )

        m_x = 0
        m_y = 0
    End Sub

    Public Overloads Sub New (x as Integer, y as Integer)

        MyBase.New ( )

        m_x = x
        m_y = y
    End Sub

End Class
```

Object constructors can accept different sets of parameters, allowing an object to be created in a particular state.

One of the more interesting things you can do with a constructor is allow the client to pass parameters to it, thereby allowing the client to place the object in a particular state immediately upon its creation. For example, the constructor of an object representing a point on a graph might accept two integer values, the X and Y location of that point. You can even have several different constructors for your class that accept different sets of parameters. For example, our point object class might have one constructor that accepts two values, another that accepts a single existing point, and yet a third that accepts no parameters and simply initializes the new point's members as zero. An example is shown in Figure 2-22. This flexibility is especially useful if you want to make an object that requires initialization before you can use it. Suppose you have an object that represents a patient in a hospital, supporting methods like *Patient.ChargeLotsOfMoney* and *Patient.Amputate (whichLimb)*. Obviously, it is vital to know which human being each individual instance of this class refers to or you might remove money or limbs from the wrong patient, both of which are bad ideas, the latter generally more so than the former. By providing a constructor that requires a patient ID—and not providing a default empty constructor—you ensure that no one can ever operate on an unidentified patient or inadvertently change a patient's ID once it's created.

Figure 2-22 *Constructor example.*

```
Dim foo As New ConstructorDemoComponent ( )

Dim bar As New ConstructorDemoComponent (4, 5)
```

.NET Memory Management

Manual memory management leads to costly, hard-to-find bugs.

One of the main sources of nasty, difficult-to-find bugs in modern applications is incorrect use of manual memory management. Older languages such as C++ required programmers to manually delete objects that they had created, which led to two main problems. First, programmers would create an object and forget to delete it when they finished using it. These leaks eventually consumed a process's entire memory space and caused it to crash. Second, programmers would manually delete an object but then mistakenly try to access its memory location later. Visual Basic would have detected the reference to invalid memory immediately, but C++ often doesn't. Sometimes the transistors that had made up the deleted object memory would still contain plausible values, and the program would continue to run with corrupted data. These mistakes seem painfully obvious in the trivial examples discussed here, and it's easy to say, "Well, just don't do that, you doofus." But in real programs, you often create an object in one part of the program and delete it in another, with complex logic intervening—logic deleting the object in some cases but not others. Both of these bugs are devilishly difficult to reproduce and harder still to track down. Programming discipline helps, of course, but we'd really like some way to keep our programmers thinking about our business logic, not about resource management. You can bet that Julia Child, the *grand dame* of TV chefs, hires someone to clean up her kitchen when she's done with it so that she can concentrate on the parts of cooking that require her unique problem-domain expertise.

Modern languages such as Visual Basic and Java don't have this type of problem. These languages feature "fire-and-forget" automatic memory management, which is one of the main reasons that programmers select them for development. A Visual Basic 6.0 programmer doesn't have to remember to delete the objects that she creates in most cases. Visual Basic 6.0 counts the references to each object and automatically deletes the object and reclaims its memory when its count reaches zero. Her development environment provides her with an automatic scullery maid cleaning the used pots and pans out of her sink and placing them back on her shelves. Wish I could get the same thing for my real kitchen. Maybe if you tell all your friends to buy this book….

Automatic memory management and resource recovery of the type built into Visual Basic and Java is a very useful feature.

Microsoft has made automatic memory management part of the .NET CLR, which allows it to be used from any language. It's conceptually simple, as shown in Figure 2-23.

Figure 2-23 *Automatic memory management with garbage collection.*

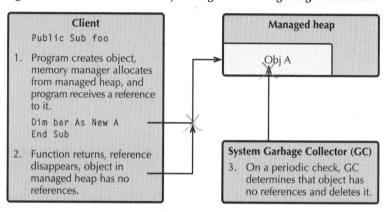

The CLR garbage collector makes automatic memory management available to any application.

A programmer creates an object using the *new* operator and receives a reference to it. The CLR allocates that object's memory from the *managed heap*, a portion of a process's memory reserved by the CLR for this purpose. Every so often, a system thread examines all the objects in the managed heap to see which of them the program still holds outstanding references to. An object to which all references have disappeared is called *garbage* and is removed from the managed heap. The objects remaining in the managed heap are then compacted together, and the existing references in the program fixed to point to their new location. The entire operation is called *garbage collection*. It solves the aforementioned problems of manual memory management without you having to write any code. You can't forget to delete an object because the system cleans up after you. And you can't access a deleted object through an invalid reference because the object won't be deleted as long as you hold any reference to it. Obviously, garbage collection is going to take more CPU cycles to run than just a standard in-out heap allocator, even though it is written to ensure that it doesn't check an object twice or get caught in circular object references. As I said previously, I think this is a good investment of CPU cycles because it gets you faster development time with fewer bugs.

This magical collection of garbage takes place when the garbage collector darn well feels like it. Apart from detecting no more available memory in the managed heap, no one really knows what the exact algorithm is for launching a garbage collection, and I guarantee you it will change many times between now and the final release of the product, and possibly from one version to another of the released product. You can force a garbage collection manually by calling the function *System.GC.Collect*. You might want to make this call at logical points in your program; for example, to clear away the debris just after a user saves a file or perhaps to clear the decks just before starting a large operation. Most of the time you just let the garbage collector do its thing when it wants to.

> The garbage collector runs when it feels like it, but you can force a garbage collection manually.

Automatic garbage collection looks great so far, but it leaves us with one gaping hole. What about the cleanup that an object needs to do when it gets destroyed? C++ applications usually cleaned up in an object's destructor, and Visual Basic classes did the same thing in their *Class_Terminate* methods. This is a good location for cleanup code because a client can't forget to call it, but how can we handle this with automatic garbage collection? First, let's realize that the problem has gotten considerably smaller. The main cleanup task we performed in C++ destructors was to delete additional objects to which the destructing object held references, and now garbage collection takes care of that for us. But occasionally we'll need to do some cleanup that doesn't involve local garbage-collected resources; for example, releasing a database connection or logging out from a remote system.

> Before garbage collection, we often put cleanup code in an object's destructor or *Class_Terminate* method.

The CLR garbage collection supports the notion of a *finalizer*, an object method that is called when the object is garbage collected. It is somewhat analogous to a C++ class destructor and also to the

Visual Basic *Class_Terminate* method, both of which it replaces. However, a finalizer is significantly different from both of these other mechanisms in ways you may find unsettling. The universal CLR base class *System.Object* contains a method called *Finalize*, which we override as shown in Figure 2-24. When the object is garbage collected, the garbage collection thread detects the fact that our object has a *Finalize* method and calls it, thereby executing our cleanup code.

Figure 2-24 *Providing a **Finalize** function in an object.*

```
Protected Overrides Sub Finalize()

    ' Perform whatever finalization logic we need.

    MessageBox.Show("In Finalize, my number = " + _
                    MyObjectNumber.ToString())

    ' Forward the call to our base class.

    MyBase.Finalize()

End Sub
```

The garbage collector supports an object finalizer method for necessary cleanup code.

WARNING

Finalizers look simple, but their behavior is actually quite complex and it's fairly easy to mess them up. If you are planning on using them, you MUST read Jeffrey Richter's two-part description of .NET garbage collection in the November and December issues of MSDN Magazine (currently online at *http://www.microsoft.com/msdnmag/*). The fact that it took him two articles to describe it should tell you something about the internal complexity of garbage collection, even if, or perhaps because, its connection to your program is simple.

Using a finalizer has some disadvantages as well. Obviously it consumes CPU cycles, so you shouldn't use it if you have no cleanup to do. There is no way to guarantee the order in which the garbage collector calls the finalizers of garbage objects, so don't depend on that. Finalizers are called on a separate garbage-collector thread, so you can't do any of your own serialization to enforce a calling order or you'll break the whole garbage collection system in your process. Finalizers are not called when an application shuts down, as the program figures that all of its internal resources will be released when the process terminates, so why bother? Early versions of .NET contained a function to allow you to force finalizers to be called on shutdown, but this has been removed from the production version. Using finalizers has other concerns as well. Read Richter's articles.

Using a finalizer can be trickier than it looks.

Finalizers are fine if we don't care when our cleanup gets done, if "eventually, by the time you really need it, I promise" is soon enough. Sometimes this is OK, but it isn't so good if the resources that a finalizer would recover are scarce in the running process—database connections, for example. Eventual recovery isn't good enough; we need this object shredded NOW so that we can recover its expensive resources that the generic garbage collector doesn't know about. We could force an immediate garbage collection, as discussed previously, but that requires examining the entire managed heap, which can be quite expensive even if there's nothing else to clean up. Since we know which object we want to dismantle, we'd like a way of cleaning up only that object, as Julia often wipes off her favorite paring knife without having to clean up her entire kitchen (including taking out the garbage). This operation goes by the grand name of *deterministic finalization*. Objects that want to support deterministic finalization do so by implementing an interface called *IDisposable*, which contains the single method, *Dispose*. In this method, you place whatever code you need to release your expensive resources. The client calls this method to tell the object to release those resources right now. An example of this is the system-provided class *System.Windows.Forms.DataGrid*. Sometimes you will see an object provide a different method name for deterministic finalization in order for the name to make sense to a developer who needs to figure out which method to call. For example, calling *Dispose* on a file object would make you think that you were shredding the file, so the developer of such an object might provide deterministic finalization through a method with the more logical name of *Close*.

Deterministic finalization sounds like a good idea, but it also contains its own drawbacks. You can't be sure that a client will remember to call your *Dispose* method, so you need to provide cleanup functionality in your finalizer as well. However, if your client does call *Dispose*, you probably don't want the garbage collector to waste its time calling your object's finalizer, as the cleanup should have already been done by the *Dispose* method. By calling the function *System.GC.SuppressFinalize*, you tell the garbage collector not to bother calling your finalizer even though you have one. Your object also needs to expressly forward the *Dispose* call to its base class if the base class contains a *Dispose* method, as the call won't otherwise get there and you will fail to release the base class's expensive resources. A sample *Dispose* method is shown in Figure 2-25. This class is derived from *System.Object*, which doesn't contain a *Dispose* method, so I've omitted the code that would forward that call.

I've written a small sample program that illustrates the concepts of automatic memory management and garbage collection. You can download it from this book's web site. A picture of the client app is shown in Figure 2-26. Note that calling *Dispose* does not make an object garbage. In fact, by definition, you can't call *Dispose* on an object that is garbage because then you wouldn't have a refer- ence with which to call *Dispose*. The object won't become gar- bage until no more references to it exist, whenever that may be. I'd suggest that your object maintain an internal flag to remember when it has been disposed of and to respond to any other access after its disposal by throwing an exception.

You have to write code to handle the case where a client accesses your object after calling *Dispose* on it.

Figure 2-25 *Sample* **Dispose** *method for deterministic finalization.*

```
Public Class Class1
    Implements System.IDisposable

    Public Sub Dispose() Implements System.IDisposable.Dispose
        ' Do whatever logic we need to do to immediately free up
        ' our resources.

        MessageBox.Show("In Dispose(), my number = " + _
                    MyObjectNumber.ToString())

        ' If our base class contained a Dispose method, we'd
        ' forward the call to it by uncommenting the following line.

        ' MyBase.Dispose()

        ' Mark our object as no longer needing finalization.

        System.GC.SuppressFinalize(Me)
    End Sub

End Class
```

Figure 2-26 *Memory Management client application.*

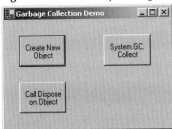

Microsoft decided on garbage collection memory management to make it leak proof, even at the cost of easy determinism.

While automatic garbage collection makes the simple operations of allocating and freeing objects easier to write and harder to mess up than they were in C++, it makes deterministic finalization harder to write and easier to mess up than it was in Visual Basic 6. C++ programmers will probably consider this a great profit, while Visual Basic programmers, who are used to their automatic, almost foolproof behavior also being deterministic, may at first consider it a step back. The reason that Microsoft switched to garbage collection is that Visual Basic's reference counting algorithm didn't correctly handle the case of circular object references, as in the case where a child object holds a reference to its parent. Suppose object A creates object B, object B creates object C, and object C obtains and holds a reference to its parent object B. B won't be destroyed when A releases its reference to it, as C still holds a reference to it. Unless a programmer writes code to break the circular reference before A lets go, both B and C are leaked away, orphans with no references except their hold on each other. The garbage collection algorithm will automatically detect and handle this circular reference case, while reference counting will not. After much discussion of alternatives and banging of heads against walls, Microsoft decided that foolproof, automatic leak prevention in all cases was more important than easy determinism. Some programmers will agree, others won't (I still haven't made up my mind, or as my architect says, I feel strongly all ways), but the choice was carefully reasoned and not capricious.

Interoperation with COM

The commercial success of any new software platform depends critically on how well it integrates with what already exists while providing new avenues for development of even better applications. For example, Windows 3.0 not only allowed existing DOS applications to run, but also multitasked them better than any other product up to that point and provided a platform for writing Windows applications that were better than any DOS app. The canvas on which we paint is essentially never blank. How did God manage to create the world in only six days? He didn't have any installed base to worry about being backward compatible with. (My editor points out that he also skimped on documentation.)

Backward compatibility is crucial in the development of any new system.

Windows has depended on COM for interapplication communication since 1993. Essentially all code for the Windows environment is neck-deep in COM and has been for an awfully long time in geek years. The .NET Framework has to support COM to have any chance of succeeding commercially. And it does, both as a .NET client using a COM server, and vice versa. Since it is more likely that new .NET code will have to interoperate with existing COM code than the reverse, I will describe that case first.

Therefore, .NET supports interoperation with COM.

Using COM Objects from .NET

A .NET client accesses a COM server by means of a *runtime callable wrapper* (RCW), as shown in Figure 2-27. The RCW wraps the COM object and mediates between it and the CLR environment, making the COM object appear to .NET clients just as if it were a native .NET object and making the .NET client appear to the COM object just as if it were a standard COM client.

A .NET client accesses a COM object through a runtime callable wrapper (RCW).

Figure 2-27 *.NET client/COM object interaction via a runtime callable wrapper.*

IUnknown, IDispatch,
IFoo interfaces

The developer of a .NET client generates the RCW in one of two ways. If you're using Visual Studio.NET, simply right-click on the References section of your project and select Add Reference from the context menu. You will see the dialog box shown in Figure 2-28, which offers a choice of all the registered COM objects it

You can generate the RCW with a variety of development tools.

finds on the system. Select the COM object for which you want to generate the RCW, and Visual Studio.NET will spit it out for you. If you're not using Visual Studio.NET, the .NET SDK contains a command line tool called TlbImp.exe, the type library importer that performs the same task. The logic that reads the type library and generates the RCW code actually lives in a .NET run-time class called *System.Runtime.InteropServices.TypeLibConverter*. Both Visual Studio.NET and TlbImp.exe use this class internally, and you can too if you're writing a development tool or feeling masochistic.

Figure 2-28   *Locating COM objects for RCW generation.*

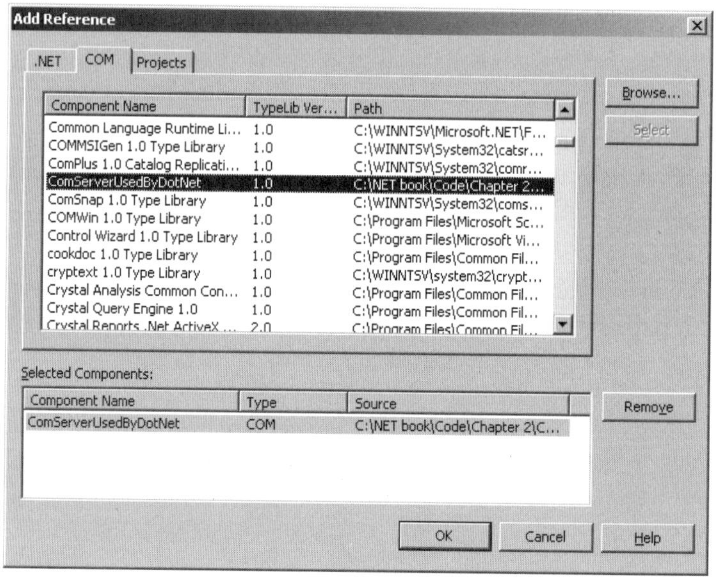

Figure 2-29 shows a sample .NET client program that uses a COM object server. You can download the samples and follow along from the book's web site. This sample contains a COM server, a COM client, and a .NET client so that you can compare the two. The source code is shown in Figure 2-30.

Figure 2-29 *Sample .NET client using a COM server.*

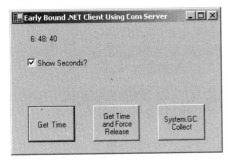

Figure 2-30 *Code listing of a .NET client using an RCW.*

```
Protected Sub Button1_Click(ByVal sender As Object, _
                            ByVal e As System.EventArgs)

    ' Create an instance of the RCW that wraps our COM object.

    Dim RuntimeCallableWrapper As New ComUsedByDotNet.Class1()

    ' Call the method that gets the time.

    Label1.Text = RuntimeCallableWrapper.GetTimeFromCom(CheckBox1.Checked)

    ' Object becomes garbage when it goes out of scope,
    ' but is not actually released until next garbage collection.

End Sub
```

After you generate the RCW as described in the preceding paragraph, you will probably want to import its namespace into the client program using the *Imports* statement, allowing you to refer to the object using its short name. You create the RCW object simply by using the *new* operator, as you would for any other .NET object. When it's created, the RCW internally calls the native COM function *CoCreateInstance*, thereby creating the COM object that it wraps. Your .NET client program then calls methods on

The RCW magically
converts .NET calls into
COM, and COM results
to .NET.

the RCW as if it were a native .NET object. The RCW automatically converts each call to the COM calling convention—for example, converting .NET strings into the BSTR strings that COM requires—and forwards it to the object. The RCW converts the results returned from the COM object into native .NET types before returning them to the client. Users of the COM support in Visual J++ will find this architecture familiar.

When you run the sample COM client program, you'll notice (from dialog boxes that I place in the code) that the object is created when you click the button and then immediately destroyed. When you run the sample .NET client program, you'll find that the object is created when you click the Get Time button, but that the object isn't destroyed immediately. You would think it should be, as the wrapper object goes out of scope, but it isn't, not even if you explicitly set the object reference to nothing. This is the .NET way of lazy resource recovery, described previously in the section about garbage collection. The RCW has gone out of scope and is no longer accessible to your program, but it doesn't actually release the COM object that it wraps until the RCW is garbage collected and destroyed. This can be a problem, as most COM objects were not written with this life cycle in mind and thus might retain expensive resources that should be released as soon as the client is finished. You can solve this problem in one of two ways. The first, obviously, is by forcing an immediate garbage collection via the function *System.GC.Collect.* Calling this function will collect and reclaim all system resources that are no longer in use, including all the RCWs not currently in scope. The drawback to this approach is that the overhead of a full garbage collection can be high, and you may not want to pay it immediately just to shred one object. If you would like to blow away one particular COM object without affecting the others, you can do so via the function *System.Runtime.InteropServices.Marshal.ReleaseComObject.*

COM objects are
actually destroyed when
their RCWs are garbage
collected.

The RCW mechanism described in the preceding paragraphs requires an object to be early-bound, by which I mean that the developer must have intimate knowledge of the object at development time to construct the wrapper class. Not all objects work this way. For example, scripting situations require late binding, in which a client reads the ProgID of an object and the method to call on it from script code at run time. Most COM objects support the *IDispatch* interface specifically to allow this type of late-bound access. Creating an RCW in advance is not possible in situations like this. Can .NET also handle it?

Fortunately, it can. The .NET Framework supports late binding to the *IDispatch* interface supported by most COM objects. A sample late binding program is shown in Figure 2-31, and its code in Figure 2-32. You create a system type based on the object's ProgID via the static method *Type.GetTypeFromProgID*. The static method *Type.GetTypeFromCLSID* (not shown) does the same thing based on a CLSID, if you have that instead of a ProgID. You then create the COM object using the method *Activator.CreateInstance* and call a method via the function *Type.InvokeMember*. It's more work—late binding always is—but you can do it.

.NET also supports late binding without too much trouble.

Figure 2-31 *Sample late binding program.*

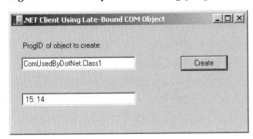

Figure 2-32 *Sample late binding code.*

```
Protected Sub Button1_Click(ByVal sender As Object, _
                            ByVal e As System.EventArgs)

    ' Get system type name based on prog ID.

    Dim MyType As System.Type
    MyType = Type.GetTypeFromProgID(textBox1().Text)

    ' Use an activator to create object of that type.

    Dim MyObj As Object
    MyObj = Activator.CreateInstance(MyType)

    ' Assemble array of parameters to pass to COM object.

    Dim prms() As Object = {checkBox1().Checked}

    ' Call method on object by its name.

    label2().Text = MyType.InvokeMember("GetTimeFromCom", _
        Reflection.BindingFlags.InvokeMethod, Nothing, MyObj, _
        prms).ToString()

End Sub
```

Using .NET Objects from COM

Suppose, on the other hand, you have a client that already speaks COM and now you want to make it use a .NET object instead. This is a somewhat less common scenario than the reverse situation that I've previously described because it presupposes new COM development in a .NET world. But I can easily see it occurring in the situation in which you have an existing client that uses 10 COM objects and you now want to add an 11th set of functionality that exists only as a .NET object—and you want all of them to look the same to the client for consistency. The .NET Framework supports this situation as well, by means of a *COM callable wrapper* (CCW), as shown in Figure 2-33. The CCW wraps up the

A COM client accesses a .NET object through a COM callable wrapper (CCW).

.NET object and mediates between it and the CLR environment, making the .NET object appear to COM clients just as if it were a native .NET object.

Figure 2-33 *COM callable wrapper.*

IUnknown, IDispatch,
IFoo interfaces

To operate with a COM-callable wrapper, a .NET component's assembly must be signed with a strong name; otherwise the CLR runtime won't be able to definitively identify it. It must also reside in the GAC, or, less commonly, in the client application's directory tree. However, as was the case previously when building the shared component's client, the component must also reside at registration time in a standard directory outside the GAC. Any .NET class that you want COM to create must provide a default constructor, by which I mean a constructor that requires no parameters. COM object creation functions don't know how to pass parameters to the objects that they create, so you need to make sure your class doesn't require this. Your class can have as many parameterized constructors as you want for the use of .NET clients, as long as you have one that requires none for the use of COM clients.

For a COM client to find the .NET object, we need to make the registry entries that COM requires. You do this with a utility program, called RegAsm.exe, that comes with the .NET SDK. This program reads the metadata in a .NET class and makes registry entries that point the COM client to it. The sample code provides a batch file that does this for you. The registry entries that it makes are shown in Figure 2-34. Notice that the COM server for this is the

A .NET component must be signed, live in the GAC, and provide a default constructor to work with a COM client.

The SDK utility RegAsm.Exe makes registry entries telling COM where to find the server for the .NET class.

intermediary DLL Mscoree.dll. The *Class* value of the *InProcServer32* key tells this DLL which .NET class to create and wrap, and the *Assembly* entry tells it in which assembly it will find this class.

Figure 2-34   Registry entries made by REGASM.EXE.

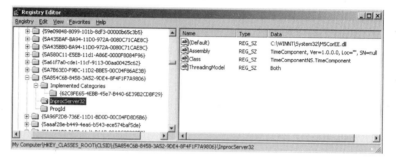

A COM client accesses a .NET object as if it were a native COM object. When the client calls *CoCreateInstance* to create the object, the registry directs the request to the registered server, Mscoree.dll. This DLL inspects the requested CLSID, reads the registry to find the .NET class to create, and rolls a CCW on the fly based on that .NET class. The CCW converts native COM types to their .NET equivalents—for example, BSTRs to .NET *Strings*—and forwards them to the .NET object. It also converts the results back from .NET into COM, including any errors. The sample code for this chapter contains a COM client that accesses the shared time component assembly that we built previously in this chapter.

The sample code for this chapter contains a COM client using a .NET object.

A .NET developer could reasonably want some methods, interfaces, or classes to be available to COM clients and others not to be. Therefore, .NET provides a metadata attribute called *System.Runtime.InteropServices.ComVisible*. You can use this attribute on an assembly, a class, an interface, or an individual method. Items marked with this attribute set to False will not be visible to COM. The default CLR setting is True, so the absence of this attribute causes the item to be visible to COM. However,

Visual Studio.NET's default behavior for assemblies is to set this attribute's value to False in the AssemblyInfo.vb file. Settings made lower in the hierarchy override those made higher up. In the sample program, I set this attribute to True on my class, thereby making it visible to COM, as shown in the code that follows. If I wanted everything in the assembly visible to COM, I'd change it in AssemblyInfo.vb.

The *ComVisible* metadata attribute specifies which portions of your .NET functionality to make available to COM clients.

```
<System.Runtime.InteropServices.ComVisible(True)> Public Class Class1
```

Transactions in .NET

Transactions are necessary to protect the integrity of data in distributed systems. Suppose we're writing an on-line bill paying application. Paying my phone bill requires us to debit my account in some database and credit the phone company's account, probably in a different database and possibly on a different machine. If the debit succeeds but the credit somehow fails, we need to undo the debit, or money would be destroyed and the integrity of the data in the system violated. We need to ensure that either both of these operations succeed or both of them fail. Performing both operations within a transaction does exactly that. If both operations succeed, the transaction commits and the new account values are saved. If either operation fails, the transaction aborts and all account values are rolled back to their original values. (To learn more about transactions in general, I highly recommend *Principles of Transaction Processing* by Philip A. Bernstein and Eric Newcomer, published by Morgan Kaufmann, 1997.)

Transactions ensure the integrity of databases during complex operations.

COM+, and its ancestor, Microsoft Transaction Server, provided automatic support that made it easy for programmers to write objects that participated in transactions. A programmer marked his objects administratively as requiring a transaction. COM+ then automatically created one when the object was activated.

COM+ contains good automatic transaction support.

The object used COM+ Resource Managers, programs such as Microsoft SQL Server that support the COM+ way of performing transactions, to make changes to a database. The object then told COM+ whether it was happy with the results. If all the objects participating in a transaction were happy, COM+ committed the transaction, telling the Resource Managers to save all their changes. If any object was unhappy, COM+ aborted the transaction, telling the Resource Managers to discard the results of all objects' operations, rolling back the state of the system to its original values. To learn more about COM+'s implementation of transactions, read my book *Understanding COM+* (Microsoft Press, 1999).

Native .NET objects can also participate in transactions. Since the existing Microsoft transaction processing system is based on COM, .NET objects do this by using their COM interoperation capability described in the previous section of this chapter. You register a .NET object as a COM server. You then use the COM+ Explorer to install that component into a COM+ application and set its transaction requirements exactly as if it were a native COM object. You can also use a command-line tool called Regsvcs.exe to perform registration and setup a COM+ application in one step. Alternatively, as a native COM component sometimes specifies its transaction requirements in its type library, you can specify a .NET object's transaction requirements in its metadata. The following code fragment shows a .NET object written in Visual Basic containing an attribute that specifies that it requires a transaction.

```
Public Class < TransactionAttribute(TransactionOption.Required) > Class1
```

If you were writing the object in C#, you'd do the same thing except you'd use square brackets instead of angle brackets. An ASP.NET page (see Chapter 3) indicates the transaction requirements of the code on it by adding attributes, as shown here.

```
<%@ page Transaction="Required" %>
```

A Web Service (see Chapter 4) indicates its transaction requirements by marking individual methods with attributes, as shown in this code snippet.

```
Public Function <WebMethod(),
    TransactionAttribute(TransactionOption.Required) > _
    HelloWorld() As String
```

A .NET object that participates in a transaction needs to vote on that transaction's outcome. You can do this in one of two ways. In COM+ and MTS, an object fetched its context by calling the API function *GetObjectContext* and then called a method on the context to indicate its transaction vote. A .NET object will find its context on the system-provided object that is named *System.EnterpriseServices.ContextUtil*. This object provides the commonly used methods *SetAbort* and *SetComplete*, and their somewhat less common siblings, *EnableCommit* and *DisableCommit*. These methods set your object's happiness and doneness bits in exactly the same manner as they did in COM+. The context also contains the properties *DeactivateOnReturn* and *MyTransactionVote*, which allow you to read and set these bits individually. Alternatively, you can make your transaction vote "fire and forget" by marking your .NET object with an attribute called *AutoComplete*. If you do this, a normal return from the object will automatically call *SetComplete*, but leaving the object by throwing an exception will automatically call *SetAbort*.

.NET objects can participate in COM+ transactions

A .NET component votes on its transaction outcome using the system-provided object *Microsoft.ComServices.ContextUtil*.

Structured Exception Handling

Every program encounters errors during its run time. The program tries to do something—open a file or create an object, for example—and the operation fails for one reason or another. How does your program find out whether an operation succeeded or failed, and how do you write code to handle the latter case?

Every program needs to handle errors that occur at run time.

The classic approach employed by a failed function is to return a special case value that indicated that failure, say, *Nothing* (or NULL in C++). This approach had three drawbacks. First, the programmer had to write code that checked the function's return value, and this often didn't happen in the time crunch that colors modern software development. Like seat belts or birth control, error-indicating return values only work if you use them. Errors didn't get trapped at their source but instead got propagated to higher levels of the program. There they were much more difficult to unravel and sometimes got masked until after a program shipped. Second, even if you were paying attention to it, the value of the error return code varied widely from one function to another, increasing the potential for programming mistakes. *CreateWindow*, for example, indicates a failure by returning 0, *CreateFile* returns −1, and in 16-bit Windows, *LoadLibrary* returned any value less than 32. To make things even more chaotic, all COM-related functions return 0 as a success code and a nonzero value to indicate different types of failures. Third, a function could only return a single value to its caller, which didn't give a debugger (human or machine) very much information to work with in trying to understand and fix the error.

Different languages tried other approaches to handling run-time errors. Visual Basic used the *On Error GoTo* mechanism, which was and is a god-awful kludge. *GoTo* has no place in modern software; it hasn't for at least a decade and maybe more. C++ and Java used a better mechanism, called *structured exception handling*, which uses an object to carry information about a failure and a handler code block to deal with that object. Unfortunately, like most features of any pre-CLR language, structured exception handling only worked within that particular language. COM tried to provide rich, cross-language exception handling through the *ISupportErrorInfo* and *IErrorInfo* interfaces, but this approach was difficult to program and you were never sure whether your counterpart was following the same rules you were.

Chapter Two

The .NET CLR provides structured exception handling, similar to that in C++ or Java, as a fundamental feature available to all languages. This architecture solves many of the problems that have dogged error handling in the past. An unhandled exception will shut down your application, so you can't ignore one during development. A function that is reporting a failure places its descriptive information in a .NET object, so it can contain any amount of information you'd like to report. Since the infrastructure is built into the CLR, you have to write very little code to take advantage of it. And as with all CLR functionality, .NET structured exception handling works well across all languages.

.NET provides structured exception handling as a fundamental feature available in and between all languages.

I've written a sample program that demonstrates some the of structured exception handling features in the CLR. Figure 2-35 shows a picture of it. You can download the code from the book's web site and work along with me.

Figure 2-35 *Sample program demonstrating structured exception handling.*

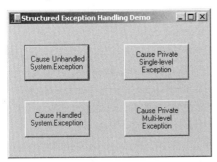

A client program about to perform an operation that it thinks might fail sets up an *exception handler* block in its code, using the keywords *Try* and *Catch*, as shown in the Visual Basic.NET code listing in Figure 2-36. The exact syntax of structured exception handling varies from one language to another, but all the ones I've seen so far are pretty close to this.

Figure 2-36 *Client application code showing structured exception handling.*

```
Protected Sub btnHandled_Click(ByVal sender As Object, _
                               ByVal e As System.EventArgs)

    ' Entering this block of code writes an exception handler onto
    ' the stack.

    Try

        ' Perform an operation that we know will cause an exception.

            Dim foo As System.IO.FileStream
            foo = System.IO.File.Open("Non-existent file", IO.FileMode.Open)


        ' When an exception is thrown at a lower level of
        ' code, this handler block catches it.

    Catch x As System.Exception

        ' Perform whatever cleanup we want to do in response
        ' to the exception that we caught.

        MessageBox.Show(x.Message)
    End Try
End Sub
```

When program execution enters the *Try* block, the CLR writes an exception handler to the stack, as shown in Figure 2-37. When a called function lower down on the stack throws an exception, as described in the next paragraph, the CLR exception-handling mechanism starts examining the stack upwards until it finds an exception handler. The stack is then unwound (all objects on it discarded), and control transfers to the exception handler. An exception can come from any depth in the call stack. In the sample program, I deliberately open a file that I know does not exist. The system method *File.Open* throws an exception, and my client catches it and displays information to the user about what has happened.

Figure 2-37 *Structured exception handling diagram.*

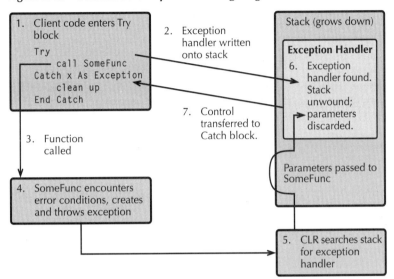

A client program uses a *Try-Catch* block to specify its exception handling code.

Any code that wants to can throw an exception. The CLR uses SEH for all of its error reporting, as shown in the previous example. For consistency, you therefore probably want to use SEH to signal errors from one part of your application to another. A piece of code that wants to throw an exception creates a new object of type *System.Exception*. You set the properties of this object to whatever you want them to be to describe the exception situation to any interested catchers. The CLR automatically includes a stack trace so that the exception handler code can tell exactly where the exception originated. Then you throw it using the keyword *Throw*, as shown in the code in Figure 2-38. This call tells the system to start examining the stack for handlers. The exception handler can live any number of levels above the exception thrower in the call stack.

A piece of code that wants to throw an exception creates a *System. Exception* object, fills out its fields, and calls the system function *Throw*.

Figure 2-38 *Throwing an exception in SEH.*

```
Public Function BottomFunction() As String

    ' Create a new Exception object, setting its "Message" property,
    ' which can only be done in the constructor.

    Dim MyException _
        As New Exception("Exception thrown by BottomFunction")

    ' Set the new Exception's Source property, which can be
    ' done anywhere.

    MyException.Source = _
        "Understanding Microsoft.NET Chapter 2 ExceptionComponent"

    ' Throw the exception.

    Throw MyException

End Function
```

When the CLR transfers control to an exception handler, the program stack between the thrower and the handler is discarded, as shown previously in Figure 2-37. Any objects or object references that existed on that stack are destroyed. Because of .NET's automatic garbage collection, you don't have to worry about objects being leaked away, which was a big concern when using C++ native exception handling. However, having the objects discarded in this manner means that you don't get a chance to call the *Dispose* methods of any that needed deterministic finalization. Their finalizers will be called eventually at the next garbage collection, but that might not be soon enough. You can handle this situation with a *Try-Finally* handler, as shown in Figure 2-39. Code in a *Finally* block is executed as the stack is unwound, so you can put your cleanup code there. You can combine a *Catch* and a *Finally* block in the same *Try* block if you want.

You can enforce cleanup from an exception using a *Try-Finally* block

Figure 2-39 *Finally handler in structured error handling.*

```
Public Function MiddleFunction() As String

    ' Entering this block causes a handler to be written onto the stack.

    Try
        BottomFunction()

        ' The code in this Finally handler is executed whenever
        ' execution leaves the Try block for any reason. We care most
        ' about the case in which BottomFunction throws an exception
        ' and the stack is unwound. Without the Finally handler, we'd
        ' have no chance to clean up from that exception.

    Finally
        MessageBox.Show("Finally handler in MiddleFunction")
    End Try

End Function
```

SEH becomes even more powerful if throwers throw different types of exceptions to indicate different types of program failure. You do this by deriving your own class from the generic base class *System.Exception*. You can add any additional methods or properties to your exception class that you think would explain the situation to any potential catchers. Even if you don't add anything else, the mere presence of a particular type of exception will indicate what type of failure has taken place. In the example shown at the start of this section, when I attempted to open the nonexistent file, the system threw an exception of type *FileNotFoundException*. I wrote the handler shown in Figure 2-35 to catch any type of exception. If I wanted the handler to catch only exceptions of the type *FileNotFoundException*, I would change *Catch x As Exception* to *Catch x As FileNotFoundException*. The CLR, when examining the stack, matches the type of exception thrown to the type specified in the *Catch* block, transferring

You can throw and catch many different types of exceptions.

control only if the type thrown matches exactly or is derived from the specified *Catch* type. A *Try* block can have any number of *Catch* handlers attached to it. The CLR will search them in the order in which they appear, so you want to put the most specific ones first.

Code Access Security

Customers generally feel that software purchased from a store is safe for them to run.

At the beginning of the PC era, very few users installed and ran code that they hadn't purchased from a store. The fact that a manufacturer had gotten shelf space at CompUSA or the late Egghead Software pretty much assured a customer that the software in the box didn't contain a malicious virus, as no nefarious schemer could afford that much marketing overhead. And, like Tylenol, the shrink wrap on the package ensured a customer that it hadn't been tampered with since the manufacturer shipped it. While the software could and probably did have bugs that would occasionally cause problems, you were fairly comfortable that it wouldn't demolish your unbacked-up hard drive just for the pleasure of hearing you scream.

However, most software today now comes from the Web.

This security model doesn't work well today because most software doesn't come from a store any more. You install some large packages, like Microsoft Office or Visual Studio, from a CD, although I wonder how much longer even that will last as high-speed Internet connections proliferate. But what about updates to, say, Internet Explorer? A new game based on Tetris? Vendors love distributing software over the Web because it's cheaper and easier than cramming it through a retail channel, and consumers like it for the convenience and lower prices. And Web code isn't limited to what you've conventionally thought of as a software application. Web pages contain scripts that do various things, not all of them good. Even Office documents that people send you by e-mail can contain scripting macros. Numerically, except for perhaps the operating system, your computer probably contains more code functions that you downloaded from the Web than you installed from a CD you purchased, and the ratio is only going to increase.

While distributing software over the Web is great from an entrepreneurial standpoint, it raises security problems that we haven't had before. It's now much easier for a malicious person to spread evil through viruses. It seems that not a month goes by without some new virus alert on CNN, so the problem is obviously bad enough to regularly attract the attention of mainstream media. Security experts tell you to run only code sent by people you know well, but who else is an e-mail virus going to propagate to? And how can we try software from companies we've never heard of? It is essentially impossible for a user to know when code downloaded from the Web is safe and when it isn't. Even trusted and knowledgeable users can damage systems when they run malicious or buggy software. You could clamp down and not let your users run any code that your IT department hasn't personally installed. Try it for a day and see how much work you get done. We've become dependent on Web code to a degree you won't believe until you try to live without it. The only thing that's kept society as we know it from collapsing is the relative scarcity of people with the combination of malicious inclination and technical skills to cause trouble.

It is essentially impossible for a user to know when Web code is safe and when it isn't.

Microsoft's first attempt to make Web code safe was its Authenticode system, introduced with the ActiveX SDK in 1996. Authenticode allowed manufacturers to attach a digital signature to downloaded controls so that the user would have some degree of certainty that the control really was coming from the person who said it was and that it hadn't been tampered with since it was signed. Authenticode worked fairly well to guarantee that the latest proposed update to Internet Explorer really did come from Microsoft and not some malicious spoofer. But Microsoft tried to reproduce the security conditions present in a retail store, not realizing that wasn't sufficient in a modern Internet world. The cursory examination required to get a digital certificate didn't assure a purchaser that a vendor wasn't malicious (like idiots, Verisign gave *me* one, for only $20), as the presence of a vendor's product on a store shelf or a mail-order catalog more or less did. Worst of all, Authenticode was an all-or-nothing deal. It told you with some degree of certainty who the code came from, but your only choice was to install it or not. Once the code was on your system, there was no way to keep it from harming you. Authenticode isn't a security system; it's an accountability system. It doesn't keep code from harming you, it just ensures that you know who to kill if it does.

> The Authenticode system doesn't protect you from harm, it merely identifies the person harming you.

> We want to specify the levels of privilege that individual pieces of code can have, as we do with the humans in our lives.

What we really want is a way to restrict the operations that individual pieces of code can perform on the basis of the level of trust that we have in that code. You allow different people in your life to have different levels of access to your resources according to your level of trust in them: a (current) spouse can borrow your credit card; a friend can borrow your older car; a neighbor can borrow your garden hose. We want our operating system to support the same sort of distinctions. For example, we might want the operating system to enforce a restriction that a control we download from the Internet can access our user interface but can't access files on our disk, unless it comes from a small set of vendors who we've learned to trust. The Win32 operating system didn't support this type of functionality, as it wasn't originally designed for this purpose. But now we're in the arms of the CLR, which is.

The .NET CLR provides *code access security*, which allows an administrator to specify the privileges that each managed code assembly has, based on our degree of trust, if any, in that assembly.

When managed code makes a CLR call to access a protected resource—say, opening a file or accessing Active Directory—the
CLR checks to see whether the administrator has granted that privilege to that assembly, as shown in Figure 2-40. The CLR walks all
the way to the top of the call stack when performing this check so
that an untrusted top-level assembly can't bypass the security system by employing trusted henchmen lower down. (If a nun attempts to pick your daughter up from school, you still want the
teacher to check that you sent her, right?) Even though this checking slows down access to a protected resource, there's no other
good way to avoid leaving a security hole. While the CLR can't
govern the actions of unmanaged code, such as a COM object,
which deals directly with the Win32 operating system instead of
going through the CLR, the privilege of accessing unmanaged
code can be granted or denied by the administrator.

Figure 2-40   *Access check in CLR code access security.*

The .NET CLR provides
code access security at
run time on a per-
assembly basis.

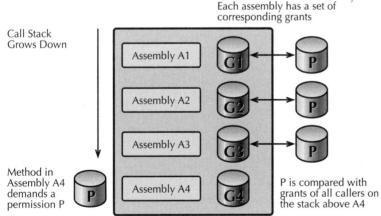

The administrator sets the *security policy,* a configurable set of
rules that says which assemblies are and which aren't allowed to

perform which types of operations. These permissions can be set at three levels: enterprise, machine, and user. A lower-level setting can tighten restrictions placed by settings at a higher level, but not the opposite. For example, if the machine-level permission allows a particular assembly to open a file, a user-level permission can deny the assembly that privilege, but not the reverse.

The administrator sets the code access security policy by editing XML-based configuration files.

An administrator sets the security policy by editing XML-based configuration files stored on a machine's disk. The exact location and internal schema of these files almost certainly will change between now and the final release of the .NET Framework. But today I find the machine-level settings in the file \WINNT\ Microsoft.NET\Framework\[current version]\machine.config. The administrator is currently expected to manipulate these files with a command line program called caspol.exe, which I find incredibly difficult to use, even by the abysmal standards of this industry. If Microsoft doesn't ship a graphical tool that's easier to use, they might as well hard-wire in the default settings because no one will ever be able to change them. To spend all that effort developing tools like IntelliSense to help programmers write applications quickly, crow about it loudly and repeatedly, and then stonewall a developer with a pig-dog "utility" like this one, is schizophrenic at best. When I saw the COM+ Explorer 2 years ago, I thought that Microsoft had finally learned its lesson about providing useful administrative tools. I guess they've forgotten again.

The administrator specifies the permissions granted to assemblies in terms of *permission sets*, which are (for once) exactly what their name implies—lists of privileges that can be granted or revoked as a unit. The default security configuration contains several permission sets, as shown in Table 2-2.

Table 2-2 Permission sets in default configuration

	Named Permission Set			
Permission	*Everything*	*Local Intranet*	*Internet*	*Nothing*
DnsPermission	All built-in unrestricted permissions, except for the Security-Permission for skipping verification.	unrestricted	—	—
Environment		USERNAME TEMP TMP	—	—
FileDialog		unrestricted (read-only access)	unrestricted (read-only access)	—
FileIO		—	—	—
Isolated Storage		AssemblyIsolation-ByUser, unrestricted quota	DomainIsolation-ByUser, 10240 bytes 365 days	—
Reflection		unrestricted	—	—
Registry		—	—	—
Security		Execution, Assertion	Execution	—
SocketPermission		connect/accept, site of origin	—	—
UI		Unrestricted	SafeSubWindows, OwnClipboard	—
WebPermission		connect, site of origin	—	—
Zone	Local (My Computer)	Intranet	Trusted Internet Sites	Restricted All Sites Code*

* Matching code groups are unioned to calculate

You can modify these or create your own permission sets if you want to. Each permission set contains one or more *permissions*. A permission is the right to do one particular thing, for example open files selected by the user in the system Open File dialog box, perhaps with a caveat that the file may be opened only for reading and not for writing. A sample of the XML describing a single permission is shown in Figure 2-41.

The administrator constructs permission sets—lists of privileges that are granted and revoked as a group.

The permission to use environment variables is unrestricted in the permission set named Everything (see section A of Figure 2-41), but it is restricted to reading the environment variables USERNAME, TEMP, and TMP in the permission set named LocalIntranet (section B of Figure 2-41). Please be advised that the set of permissions and their internal XML structure is exactly the sort of thing that is most vulnerable to change between the writing of this book and the final release of the software.

An administrator assigns permission sets to code groups.

Now that you know which sets of permissions are available to the administrator, we need to look at how the administrator assigns a permission set to an assembly. A code-privilege administrator can assign a permission set to a specific assembly just as a log-in administrator can assign specific log-in privileges to an individual user. Both of these techniques, however, become unwieldy very quickly. Most log-in administrators set up user groups (workers, officers, and so on), the members of which share a common level of privilege, and move individual users into and out of the groups. In a similar manner, most code-privilege administrators will set up groups of assemblies, known as *code groups*, and assign permission sets to these groups. The main difference between a log-in administrator's task and a code-privilege administrator's task is that the former will deal with each user's group membership manually, as new users come onto the system infrequently. Because of the way code is downloaded from the Web, we can't rely on a human to make a trust decision every time our browser encounters a new code assembly. A code-privilege administrator, therefore, sets up rules, known as *membership conditions*, that determine how assemblies are assigned to the various code groups. A membership condition will usually include the program zone that an assembly came from, for example, My Computer, Internet, Intranet, and so on. A membership condition can also include such information as the strong name of the assembly ("our developers wrote it"), or the public key with which it was signed ("Microsoft wrote it"). When the CLR loads an assembly at run time, it figures out which code group the assembly belongs to by checking its membership conditions and assigns it the permission set specified for that code group. Figure 2-42 shows an excerpted version of the complex XML that specifies that assemblies originating in the My Computer zone are assigned the FullTrust permission set. See what I mean about needing good administrative tools?

An administrator sets the rules for assembly membership in a code group.

Figure 2-41 *Excerpted XML describing a single permission.*

A) Permission for unrestricted access to all environment variables

```
<Permission class="System.Security.Permissions.EnvironmentPermission">
    <Unrestricted/>
</Permission>
```

B) Permission for read-only access the USERNAME, TEMP, and TMP variable

```
<Permission class="System.Security.Permissions.EnvironmentPermission">
    <Read>USERNAME;TEMP;TMP</Read>
</Permission>
```

Figure 2-42 *Excerpted XML showing code group and membership condition for granting FullTrust permission set.*

```
<ICodeGroup class="System.Security.Policy.UnionCodeGroup">
    <IMembershipCondition class=
        "System.Security.Policy.ZoneMembershipCondition">
        <Zone>MyComputer</Zone>
    </IMembershipCondition>
    <PermissionSet class="System.Security.NamedPermissionSet">
        <Name>FullTrust</Name>
    </PermissionSet>
</ICodeGroup>
```

The CLR contains many functions and objects for interaction with the code-access security system programmatically.

While most of the effort involved in code access security falls on system administrators, programmers will occasionally need to write code that deals with the code-access security system. For example, a programmer might want to add metadata attributes to an assembly specifying the permission set that it needs to get its work done. This doesn't affect the permission level it will get, as that's controlled by the administrative settings I've just described, but it will allow the CLR to fail its load immediately instead of waiting for the assembly to try an operation that it's not allowed to do. On the other hand, perhaps some uses of the assembly require forbidden operations and others don't, in which case you wouldn't want this. A programmer might also want to read the level of permission that an assembly actually has been granted so that it can inform the user or an administrator what it's missing. The CLR contains many functions and objects that allow programmers to write code that interacts with the code-access security system. Even a cursory examination of them is far beyond the scope of this book, but you should know that they exist, that you can work with them if you want to, and that you almost never will want to. If you set the administrative permissions the way I've just described, the right assemblies will be able to do the right things, and the wrong assemblies will be barred from doing the wrong things.

Note

As I was reviewing page proofs the week before this book went to press, Microsoft announced that it has caved in to intense pressure from Visual Basic developers and changed the operation of arrays in Visual Basic again. Arrays will still be zero-based, but Visual Basic.NET will automatically allocate an extra element at the top of the array so that you don't have to rewrite all of your existing array code. When you say *Dim X(5) As Integer,* you'll actually get 6 elements, numbered 0 through 5. This means that existing Visual Basic code won't have to be changed to run on its own.

The problem is that now, when you share Visual Basic code with zero-based languages like C# or Java, the other developer will know that element 0 is indeed present, but he won't know whether you put anything in it. The one-based/zero-based code interchange problem, whose demise I was deliciously anticipating, has been deliberately given a new lease on life. It would have been far better to bite the bullet and get it done once, consistently. Maybe Microsoft is playing Solomon, hoping the zero-based developers will now fall on their knees, saying "No! Anything but that mass confusion. Make them all one-based, we surrender!" I hope this change is overturned on appeal.

```vb
                    'CODEGEN: This procedure is required by the WebServices Designer
                    'Do not modify it using the code editor.
                    InitializeComponent()

                    'Add your own initialization code after the InitializeComponent
                    'call
                End Sub

        Private Sub InitializeComponent()
                'CODEGEN: This procedure is required by the WebServices Designer
                'Do not modify it using the code editor.
                components = New System.ComponentModel.Container()
            End Sub


            Overrides Sub Dispose()
                'CODEGEN: This
```

`#End Region`

`<WebMethod()> P                    ByVal ShowSe`
`                                        As String`

`If 'C`

Chapter Three

ASP.NET

Interdependence absolute, foreseen, ordained, decreed,
To work, Ye'll note, at any tilt an' every rate o' speed.
Fra skylight-lift to furnace-bars, backed, bolted, braced an' stayed,
An' singin' like the Mornin' Stars for joy that they are made;

—Rudyard Kipling, writing on interoperation and
scalability, "McAndrew's Hymn," 1894.

Problem Background

The Web was first used to deliver static pages of text and pictures. Programming a server to do this was relatively easy—just accept the URL identifying the file, fetch the file that it names from the server's disk, and write that file back to the client, as shown in Figure 3-1. You can do a lot with just this simple architecture. For example, my local art cinema has a small Web site that I can browse to see what's playing tonight (most recently *Happy, Texas*, in which two escaped convicts are mistaken for beauty pageant organizers in a small Texas town), learn about coming attractions, and follow links to trailers and reviews. They're using the Web like a paper brochure, except with richer content, faster delivery, and lower marginal cost—in a word, lower friction. (OK, two words, I was off by one.)[1]

---

1 One of the smartest, albeit geekiest, guys I know once said that there's only one bug in all of computing, and it's being "off by one." "Can't you be off by 25,000?" I asked him. "You've got to be off by one first," he replied.

The Web was initially used for viewing static pages, which was relatively easy to program.

Figure 3-1   *Server delivering static Web pages.*

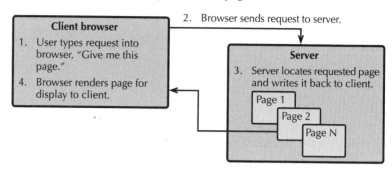

This approach worked well in the prehistoric days when all data on the Web was static (rendering the author's content verbatim, with no user input or programming logic) and public (available to anyone who knew or could find the magic address). But customers soon started asking, "If I can see what movie's playing tonight, why can't I see my current bank balance?" which the static page approach can't handle. A bank can't create a new page every day for every possible view of every account—there are far too many of them. Instead, the user needs to provide input such as the account number, and the bank's computer needs to create on demand an HTML page showing the user's account balance, as shown in Figure 3-2. This data is neither static nor public, which raises thorny new design problems

Web programmers today need to dynamically generate HTML pages in response to input received from the user, which poses new problems.

Figure 3-2   *Server dynamically generating Web pages based on client input.*

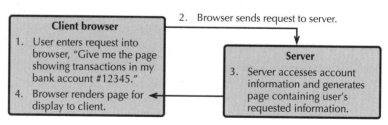

A Web server application that dynamically generates pages for a client needs several things. First, it needs a way of associating some sort of program logic with a page request. When a user requests a page, the server doesn't simply fetch the page from the disk; the page doesn't exist before the request. Instead, the server executes program logic that generates the page. In the bank example, we probably need to do a database lookup in the bank's central ledger to find out the customer's current balance and recent transactions. We'd like to be able to write this logic quickly and easily, using languages and tools with which we are already familiar. And we'd like it to run as quickly and efficiently as possible in production.

Our Web server application requires program logic that generates pages.

Second, our Web server needs a way to get input from the user into the server-side program logic and output from that program logic back to the user. The user's browser submits to the server an HTML form, whose input controls specify the data that he'd like to see on his page—for example, his account number and the range of dates for which he wants to see transactions. Parsing the interesting data values from this HTML is tedious and highly repetitive, so we'd like a prefabricated way of doing it that's quick and easy for us to program. Think how much easier the text box (edit control for you C++ geeks) makes reading character input in a Windows user interface compared to assembling character strings yourself from individual keystrokes. We'd also like a similar level of prefabrication in assembling the HTML page for output to the user. Raw HTML is difficult and tedious to write. Think how much easier the label control makes output in a Windows user interface compared to writing all the GDI calls needed to set font, color, text, and so on. We'd like something similar for the HTML output that a browser requires.

Our Web server needs a convenient way of receiving input from and writing output to the user's browser.

Our Web server needs security services to keep unauthorized users from seeing or doing things that they shouldn't.

Third, since at least some of our data is now private, our Web server needs to make sure that we know who a user is and that we only allow the user to see and do the things that he's allowed to. You'd like to see your bank account, but you really don't want your disgruntled former spouse looking at it, or, far worse, moving money out of it. This type of code is notoriously difficult and expensive to write—and proving to your wary customers that you've made the code bulletproof is equally difficult and expensive. We need a prefabricated infrastructure that provides these security services to us.

Our Web server needs a way to manage user sessions.

Finally, our Web server needs a mechanism for managing user sessions. A user doesn't think of her interaction with a Web site in terms of individual page requests. Instead, she thinks of it in terms of a conversation, a "session," that takes place over some reasonable amount of time. She expects the Web site to be able to remember things that she's told it a few minutes previously. For example, a user expects to be able to place items in an e-commerce site's shopping cart and have the cart remember these items until check out. Individual page requests don't inherently do this; we have to write the code ourselves to make it happen. Again, it's an integral part of most Web applications, so we'd like a prefabricated implementation of it that's easy to use. Ideally, it would work correctly in a multiserver environment and survive crashes.

We need an entire Web server programming and run-time environment.

In short, our Web server needs a run-time environment that provides prefabricated solutions to the programming problems common to all Web servers. We'd like it to be easy to program as well as to administer and deploy. We'd like it to scale to at least a few servers, ideally more. And we don't want to pay a lot for it. Not asking for much, are we?

Solution Architecture

Microsoft released a relatively simple Web run-time environment called Active Server Pages (ASP) as part of Internet Information Server (IIS), itself part of the Windows NT 4 Option Pack in the fall of 1997. IIS served up Web pages requested by the user. ASP allowed programmers to write program logic that dynamically constructed the pages that IIS supplied by mixing static HTML and scripting code, as shown in Figure 3-3. When a client requested an ASP page, IIS would locate the page and activate the ASP processor. The ASP processor would read the page and copy its HTML elements verbatim to an output page. In this case, the *style* attribute sets the text color to blue. It would also interpret the scripting elements, located within the delimiters <% %>. This code would perform program logic that rendered HTML strings as its output, which the ASP processor would copy to the location on the output page where the scripting element appeared. The resulting page, assembled from the static HTML elements and HTML dynamically generated by the script, would be written back to the client, as shown in Figure 3-4. ASP was relatively easy to use for simple tasks, which is the hallmark of a good first release.

The original ASP was a Web server run-time environment that was easy to use for simple tasks.

Figure 3-3   Intermingling of code and HTML in ASP.

```
<html style="color:#0000FF;">
    The time is:  <% =time %> on <% =date %>
</html>
```

Figure 3-4   The Web page produced by ASP after processing the HTML/ code mixture in Figure 3-3.

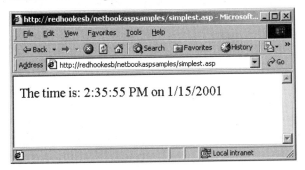

ASP.NET is a complete rewrite of the original ASP, keeping the best concepts.

As the Web spread and user demands increased, Web programmers required more sophistication from their Web run-time environment in two key areas: making it easier to program and making it run better. ASP.NET is a big improvement in both these areas. ASP.NET looks somewhat like the original ASP, and most code will port between the versions unchanged or very close to it. But internally ASP.NET has been completely redone to take advantage of the .NET Framework. You'll find that it runs better, crashes less, and is easier to program. These are good things to have. I discuss all of these features in more depth later in this chapter.

ASP's mingling of HTML output elements and scripting code may look logical, but it's the devil to program and maintain in any but the simplest cases. Because code and data could and did appear anywhere on the page, intelligent development environments such as Visual Basic couldn't make sense of it, so no one ever wrote a development environment that could handle ASP well. This meant that ASP code was harder to write than other types of code, such as a Visual Basic user interface application using forms. I know it drove me bats.

ASP.NET disentangles your code from the HTML.

ASP.NET separates the HTML output from the program logic using a feature called *code-behind*. Instead of mixing HTML and code, you write the code in a separate file to which your ASP page contains a reference. You'd be astounded how much easier your code is to understand when you remove the distraction of HTML output syntax. It's like getting your three-year old to shut up while you're talking taxes on the phone with your accountant. Because of this separation, Microsoft was able to enhance the Visual Studio.NET programming and debugging environment so that you can use it while developing your Web applications.

Input and output in original ASP could be tricky, as the HTML environment was imperfectly abstracted. By this I mean that the programmer often had to spend time grappling with some fairly grotty

HTML language constructs instead of thinking about her program logic, which isn't the best use of resources. For example, parsing data out of HTML forms required much more work than doing the same thing on a desktop app. Producing output required the programmer to assemble HTML output streams, which again isn't where you want your programmers to be spending their time. In Figure 3-3, our programmer had to know the proper HTML syntax for turning the text color blue.

ASP.NET supports *Web Forms*, which is a Web page architecture that makes programming a Web page very similar to programming a desktop application form. You add controls to the page and write handlers for their events, just as you do when writing a desktop app in Visual Basic. The ease of use that made Visual Basic so popular is now available for constructing Web applications. Just before this book went to press, I taught a class on the beta 1 release of ASP.NET to a seasoned bunch of ASP developers, and this is the feature that made them literally stand up and cheer.

As Visual Basic depended on Windows controls and third-party ActiveX controls, so does Web Forms depend on a new type of control, named *Web Forms Server Controls*. For convenience, I refer to these as Web controls in this chapter. These are pieces of prefabricated logic dealing with input and output that a designer places on ASP.NET pages, just as he did with a Windows application form. The controls abstract away the details of dealing with HTML, just as Windows controls did for the Windows GDI. For example, you no longer have to remember the HTML syntax for setting the foreground and background color for a line of text. Instead, you'll use a label control and write code that accesses the control's properties, just as you did in any other programming language. Think of how easy controls make it for you to program a simple desktop app in Visual Basic. Web controls do the same thing for ASP.NET pages.

ASP.NET contains prefabricated controls that do for HTML pages what Windows controls did for Windows applications.

ASP.NET contains much good prefabricated support for securing your applications.

Original ASP included very little support for security programming. Security in ASP.NET is much easier to write. If you're running in a Windows-only environment, you can authenticate a user (verify that he really is who he says he is) automatically using Windows built-in authentication. For the majority of installations that are not Windows-only, ASP.NET contains prefabricated support for writing your own authentication scheme. And it also contains prefabricated support for Microsoft's Passport worldwide authentication initiative, if you decide to go that route.

ASP.NET contains new Web farmable session state management features.

Original ASP supported session state management with an easy-to-use API. Its main drawbacks were that the state management couldn't expand to more than one machine and that it couldn't survive a process restart. ASP.NET expands this support by adding features that allow it to do both automatically. You can set ASP.NET to automatically save and later restore session state either to a designated server machine—if you want it to scale to more than one machine but don't care about persistence—or to Microsoft SQL Server.

ASP.NET contains many features, making it run better and making it easier to administer.

ASP.NET contains many useful new run-time features as well. Original ASP executed rather slowly because the scripting code on its pages was interpreted at run time. ASP.NET automatically compiles pages, either when a page is installed or when it's first requested, which makes it run much faster. Because it uses the .NET Framework's just-in-time compilation, you don't have to stop the server to replace a component or a page. It also supports recycling of processes. Instead of keeping a process running indefinitely, ASP.NET can be set to automatically shut down and restart its server process after a configurable time interval or number of hits. This solves most problems of memory leaks in user code. ASP.NET also has the potential of being easier to administer because all settings are stored in human-readable files in the ASP directory hierarchy itself. Unfortunately, the administrative tools that would make this job easier are still under development at the time of this writing.

Simplest Example: Writing a Simple ASP.NET Page

Let's look at the simplest ASP.NET example that I could think of. Shown in Figure 3-5, it displays the current time on the server, either with or without the seconds digits, in the user's choice of text color. You can download the code from this book's Web site, *www.introducingmicrosoft.net*, and follow along with the discussion. You will also find this page on the Web site, so you can open it in your browser and observe its behavior while I describe what I did to make it work that way. You can also easily set up the page on your own ASP.NET server.

Figure 3-5   *Simplest example of ASP.NET.*

An ASP.NET sample program begins here.

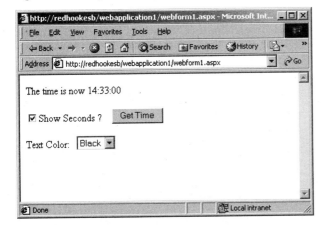

I wrote this sample using Visual Studio.NET. While I've tried to write my examples in a tool-agnostic manner, Visual Studio.NET contains so much built-in support for ASP.NET that not using it would have been like using Notepad to write a Visual Basic Windows desktop app. You can do it if you really, REALLY want to and probably get it to work eventually. But it will be much faster and less painful if you take the right approach from the beginning.

The key to understanding this example is to think of your Web page as a Visual Basic form. I use that analogy because I think that my readers are most familiar with it, but you could write this same code in any other Visual Studio.NET language—C#, C++, or JScript—if you want to. I started by generating a Web Application project from Visual Studio.NET, as shown in Figure 3-6. Doing this creates, among other things, an ASP.NET page called WebForm1.aspx. I then used the Toolbox to drag Web controls onto the form, shown in Figure 3-7, adding a check box, a button, a drop-down list, and a couple of labels. I then set the properties of these controls using the Properties window in the lower right corner of the Visual Studio.NET window, specifying the text of each control, the font size of the labels, and the items in my drop-down list collection. I set the *AutoPostBack* property of the drop-down list control to True, meaning that it automatically posts the form back to the server when the user makes a new selection in the drop-down list. It's easy to do, you get it done fast, and you get it done right.

Figure 3-6 *Choosing a Web Application in Visual Studio.NET.*

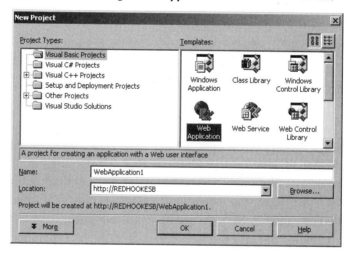

Figure 3-7 *Using the Toolbox to drag Web controls onto the form.*

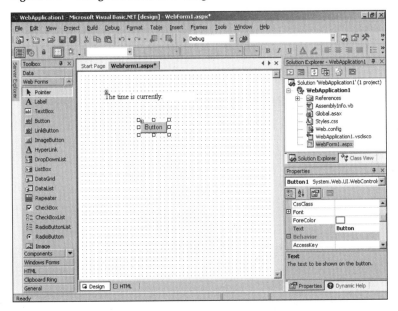

You put Web controls on your .ASPX pages, just as you do on a Visual Basic form.

Now that I've laid out my controls, I need to write the code that ties them together. When I generated the project, Visual Studio.NET also generated the class that represents the code behind my ASP.NET page. You view it by right-clicking on the page and selecting View Code from the shortcut menu, just as you do today with forms in Visual Basic 6.0. Web controls fire events to their forms, again just as in Visual Basic, so I need to write event handlers for them. I can add an event handler by choosing the control from the upper-left drop-down list and see the events in the upper-right drop-down box. I show excerpts from my Visual Basic class in Figure 3-8, and all of it is included with this book's downloadable sample code. In this simple example, when the button reports a *Click* event, I change the label's text property to hold the current time. I also added a handler for my drop-down list box's *SelectedIndexChanged* event. When the user makes a color selection from the list box, I set the label's color to the value selected by the user. When I build the project, Visual Studio.NET automatically publishes it to my machine's Web root directory.

Figure 3-8 *Excerpts from the code behind the WebForm1.aspx page.*

```
Public Class WebForm1
    Inherits System.Web.UI.Page


    ' User clicked the button. Fetch the time and display it in the
    ' label control.

    Public Sub Button1_Click(ByVal sender As Object, _
                            ByVal e As System.EventArgs) _
        If CheckBox1.Checked = True Then
            Label1.Text = "The time is now " + now.ToLongTimeString
        Else
            Label1.Text = "The time is now " + now.ToShortTimeString
        End If
    End Sub



    ' User has selected a different color from the list box.
    ' Change the label's color to reflect the user's choice.


    Protected Sub DropDownList1_SelectedIndexChanged(ByVal sender _
            As System.Object, _
            ByVal e As System.EventArgs) _
            Handles DropDownList1.SelectedIndexChanged
        Label1().ForeColor = Color.FromName(DropDownList1().SelectedItem.Text)
    End Sub

End Class
```

You write event handlers for your controls' events, just as you do for a Visual Basic form.

Now that I've finished writing my code, I'd like to see it in action. The easiest way to do this is to right-click on the page and select Build and Browse from the shortcut menu. This opens a browser window within the Visual Studio.NET environment. When this browser (or any other client) requests the .ASPX page, IIS loads it into the ASP.NET execution engine, which then parses the page. The first time the engine encounters the page it compiles its code "just-in-time." Subsequent requests for the same page will load and run the compiled code. The engine then executes the class's compiled code, creating the Web controls that I earlier placed on the form. The controls run only on the server side, rendering HTML that reflects their current state, which is incorporated in the page that gets sent to the client. The engine also executes the event handlers' code and renders the output HTML created by the code's interaction with the controls. The final HTML is written back to the client, which produces the page shown previously in Figure 3-5.

An execution engine executes the class associated with the ASP.NET page and renders HTML from its controls and code.

That's all I had to do to write an .ASPX page using Visual Studio.NET and Web controls. It's much easier than original ASP. It looks like and feels like writing Visual Basic code, which we're already comfortable and familiar with.

More on Web Controls

Web controls spring from the same philosophy that led to the creation of Windows user interface controls 15 years ago. That architecture made Bill Gates the world's richest man (at the time of this writing, although maybe not much longer if the stock market keeps going down). That's my definition of a successful architecture; don't know about yours.

Input and output operations are highly repetitive. Prefabricating them—rolling them up in a capsule for any programmer to use—is a great idea. You kids today don't know how lucky you are not to have to worry about writing your own button controls, for example, and painting the pixels differently to make the button look as if it's been clicked. This not only saves an enormous amount of expensive programming time, but also makes every program's user interface more consistent and thus easier for users to understand. Remember (I'm dating myself here) Windows 3.0, which didn't contain a standard File Open dialog box? Every application programmer had to roll her own. It cost a lot, and every

Controls exist to encapsulate reusable program logic dealing with user interfaces.

application's implementation looked and worked a little (or a lot) differently. Windows 3.1 provided a File Open dialog box as part of the operating system, which made the lives of programmers and users much easier. A Web control, in the ASP.NET sense of the word, is any type of user-interface-related programming logic that is capable of a) exposing a standard programming model to a development environment such as Visual Studio.NET, and b) rendering its appearance into HTML for display in a standard browser—more or less as a Windows control renders its appearance into Windows GDI function calls.

Web controls are richer, more numerous, and easier to program than standard HTML controls.

"But HTML already *has* controls," you say. "Buttons and checkboxes and links. I use them all the time. Why do I have to learn a new set?" HTML does support a few controls as part of the language, but these have severe limitations. First, they're not very numerous or very rich. A text box and a drop-down list box are about as far as they go. Compare their number to the controls advertised in *Visual Basic Programmers Journal* or their functionality to Visual Basic's data-bound grid control. We'd like to be able to package a lot more functionality than the few and wimpy existing HTML elements provide. Second, they are hard to write code for. The communication channel between an HTML control and its run-time environment isn't very rich. The Web Forms environment that Web controls inhabit contains an event-driven programming model similar to Visual Basic. It's much easier to program, there's much better support in development environments, and it abstracts away many of the differences from one browser to another. Web controls do more and are easier to program. Sounds decisive to me.

Web controls exist for many different functions.

ASP.NET comes with the set of basic Web controls listed in Table 3-1. I expect that once the programming model is released, third-party vendors will develop and market Web controls for every conceivable type of situation, as happened with ActiveX controls. You can also write your own, which isn't very hard (although, regrettably, beyond the scope of at least this edition of this book).

Table 3-1   Web Forms Server Controls by Function

Function	Control	Description
Text display (read only)	Label	Displays text that users can't directly edit.
Text edit	TextBox	Displays text entered at design time that can be edited by users at run time or changed programmatically.
		Note: Although other controls allow users to edit text (for example, DropDownList), their primary purpose is not usually text editing.
Selection from a list	DropDownList	Allows users to either select from a list or enter text.
	ListBox	Displays a list of choices. Optionally, the list can allow multiple selections.
Graphics display	Image	Displays an image.
	AdRotator	Displays a sequence (predefined or random) of images.
Value setting	CheckBox	Displays a box that users can click to turn an option on or off.
	RadioButton	Displays a single button that can be selected or not.
Date setting	Calendar	Displays a calendar to allow users to select a date.
Commands	Button	Used to perform a task.
	LinkButton	Like a Button control but has the appearance of a hyperlink.
	ImageButton	Like a Button control but incorporates an image instead of text.

(continued)

(continued)

Function	Control	Description
Navigation controls	HyperLink	Creates Web navigation links.
Table controls	Table	Creates a table.
	TableCell	Creates an individual cell within a table row.
	TableRow	Creates an individual row within a table.
Grouping other controls	CheckBoxList	Creates a collection of check boxes.
	Panel	Creates a borderless division on the form that serves as a container for other controls.
	RadioButtonList	Creates a group of radio buttons. Inside the group, only one button can be selected.
List controls	Repeater	Displays information from a data set using a set of HTML elements and controls that you specify, repeating the elements once for each record in the data set.
	DataList	Like the Repeater control but with more formatting and layout options, including the ability to display information in a table. The DataList control also allows you to specify editing behavior.
	DataGrid	Displays information, usually data-bound, in tabular form with columns. Provides mechanisms to allow editing and sorting.

When I placed controls on my form in the preceding example, Visual Studio.NET generated the statements in the .ASPX page, shown in Figure 3-9. Every statement that starts with *<asp: >* is a directive to the ASP.NET parser to create a control of the specified type when it generates the class file for the page. For example, in response to the statement *<asp:label>*, the parser creates a label control in the class. When the page is executed, the ASP.NET execution engine executes the event handler code on the page that interacts with the controls (fetching the time and setting the text and background color, as shown previously in Figure 3-8). Finally, the engine tells each control to render itself into HTML in accordance with its current properties, just as a Windows control renders itself into GDI calls in accordance with its current properties. The engine then writes the resulting HTML to the client's browser. Figure 3-10 shows this process schematically. Excerpts from the actual HTML sent to the client are shown in Figure 3-11.

The execution engine creates and uses the controls on the server side.

The controls render their own HTML for the client.

Figure 3-9 *Excerpts from .ASPX page created by Visual Studio.NET, showing control statements.*

```
<%@ Page Language="vb" AutoEventWireup="false" Codebehind="WebForm1.aspx.vb"
    Inherits="WebApplication1.WebForm1"%>

<html>
    <body>
        <form id="WebForm1" method="post" runat="server">

<asp:Label id=Label1 runat="server" forecolor="Black">
    (time will be displayed here)
</asp:Label></p>

<asp:CheckBox id=CheckBox1 runat="server" Text="Show Seconds ?"/>
<asp:Button id=Button1 runat="server" Text="Get Time" />

<asp:DropDownList id=DropDownList1 runat="server" autopostback="True">
    <asp:ListItem Value="Black" Selected="True">Black</asp:ListItem>
    <asp:ListItem Value="Red">Red</asp:ListItem>
    <asp:ListItem Value="Green">Green</asp:ListItem>
    <asp:ListItem Value="Blue">Blue</asp:ListItem>
</asp:DropDownList></p>

        </form>
    </body>
</html>
```

Figure 3-10 *.ASPX page execution engine sequence.*

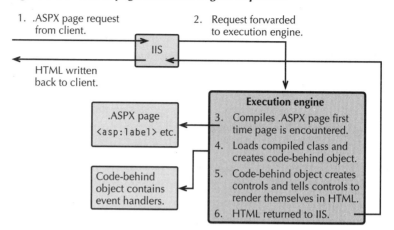

Figure 3-11 *Excerpts from the HTML generated by the controls.*

```
<span id="Label1" style="color:Black;">
    (time will be displayed here)
</span>

<span>
<input type="checkbox" id="CheckBox1" name="CheckBox1" />
<label for="CheckBox1">Show Seconds ?</label>
</span>

<input type="submit" name="Button1" value="Get Time" id="Button1" />

<p>Text Color:

<select name="DropDownList1" id="DropDownList1"
        onchange="javascript:__doPostBack('DropDownList1','')">
    <option selected value="Black">Black</option>
    <option value="Red">Red</option>
    <option value="Green">Green</option>
    <option value="Blue">Blue</option>
</select>
```

Another great feature of the input controls in the Web controls package (list box, text box, check box, radio button, and so on) is that they can automatically remember the state in which the user left them when the page they are on makes a round-trip to the server. Microsoft calls this feature *postback data*. For example, suppose a server sends a page to a browser containing a check box that is empty. Suppose then that the browser's human user checks the box and posts the form back to the server. If the server processed the form and sent the same form back to the client, the check box wouldn't automatically remember its checked state. Instead, the server developer would have to write code to make sure that the state of the check box it was sending back to the client matched the one that the client had submitted. You don't have to write this code for input Web controls; they automatically remember their previous state within a user session. (I'll describe this in more detail later in this chapter.) The data is actually stored in a dedicated field in the HTTP header. This is an automatic feature that you can't turn off.

Input controls can maintain their contents and selection from one round-trip to another.

The display controls in the Web controls package, such as label, data list, data grid, and repeater, support their own version of property retention, called *view state*. Even though the user doesn't set them to specific values, they still remember the state in which the program left them in the previous round trip. The .ASPX page environment automatically places a hidden input control called _ _VIEWSTATE on each of its pages. Web controls automatically serialize their state into this hidden control when the page is being destroyed and then retrieve their state when the page is next created, which is what you want most of the time. If you don't want this, you easily can turn it off by setting the control's *MaintainState* property to False.

Display controls can also maintain their state from one round-trip to another.

Why did Microsoft use two separate mechanisms for maintaining control state, one for input controls and the other for display controls? Probably to make it easier for programmers to comply with the Principle of Least Astonishment, which states simply that astonishing a human user is not a good thing, therefore you should do it as seldom as possible. When a user types something into a field, she expects to see what she typed stay there until she does something that changes it. If an input control didn't automatically maintain its state, a developer would have to write code to make it do so or astonish the heck out of his users. Since you have to do this all the time, Microsoft built it into the input control behavior and didn't provide an off switch. On the other hand, a display control doesn't display what a user typed in. Instead, it usually shows the results of a computing operation. Sometimes you might want a display control to remember its state between operations, and sometimes you might not. Hence a different mechanism, this one with an off switch.

Web controls can also discover the specific browser on which the user will be viewing the page so that they can render their HTML to take advantage of different browser features if they want to. A good example of this is the range validator control, shown in Figure 3-12. Ensuring that a user-entered number falls between a certain maximum and minimum value is such a common task that Microsoft provides a Web control for it. You place the control on a form and set properties that tell it which text box to validate and what the maximum and minimum values are. When the control renders its HTML, it checks the version of the browser it's running on. If it's a newer browser that supports DHTML (specifically MSDOM 4.0 or later, and EcmaScript version 1.2 or later), the control renders HTML that includes a client-side script that will perform the numeric validation in the user's browser before submitting the form to the server, thereby avoiding a network round-trip if a control contains invalid data. If all the data passes validation on the client, the form is submitted to the server. Somewhat counterintuitively, the validation operation is then repeated on the server, even though it passed on the client. This guarantees that the validation is performed before your serverside code runs, even if the control somehow messed up the client-side script on a flaky browser. If the control detects an older browser that doesn't support DHTML, it automatically generates HTML code that performs a round-trip and validates on the server.

Figure 3-12 *The range validator control.*

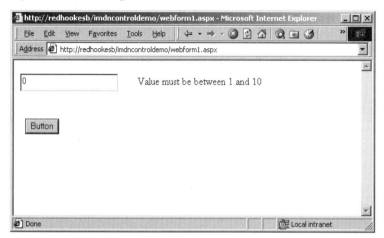

Web controls can detect the capabilities of the browser they are running on and render different code to take advantage of them.

Writing your own Web controls isn't that hard because the .NET Framework contains prefabricated base classes from which you can inherit most of your control's necessary infrastructure (sort of like MFC on steroids). An example, unfortunately, is beyond the scope of this book, at least this edition.

You can write your own Web controls without too much trouble.

Managing and Configuring Web Application Projects: The Web.config File

A powerful run-time environment like ASP.NET provides many prefabricated services. As you can imagine, an individual application has many, many options for its configuration. The configuration mechanism of an environment is as important as the underlying software that it controls. Cool features that you can't configure, or can't figure out how to configure, are about as useful as Bill Clinton's marriage vows.

A powerful run-time environment like ASP.NET requires excellent configuration management.

WARNING: The details described in this section are more subject to change in future releases than most of what I describe in this book.

ASP.NET keeps its configuration information in individual files, each having the name web.config.

Previous run-time environments have used a central store for their configuration information. For example, classic COM used the system registry and COM+ added the COM+ catalog. ASP.NET takes a different, decentralized approach. Each application stores its ASP.NET configuration management information in a file named web.config, which is stored in the application's own directory. Each file contains configuration information expressed in a particular XML vocabulary. Excerpts from our sample program's web.config file are shown in Figure 3-13. This excerpt shows the compilation and custom error handling settings of this particular application. I will discuss other settings later in this chapter.

Figure 3-13 *Excerpts from the sample application's web.config file.*

```
<?xml version="1.0" encoding="utf-8" ?>
<configuration>

    <system.web>

        <!--   DYNAMIC DEBUG COMPILATION
            Set compilation debug="true" to enable ASPX debugging.
            Otherwise, setting this value to false will improve
            runtime performance of this application.
        -->
        <compilation defaultLanguage="vb" debug="true" />

        <!--   CUSTOM ERROR MESSAGES
            Set customErrors mode="On" or "RemoteOnly" to enable
            custom error messages, "Off" to disable. Add <error>
            tags for each of the errors you want to handle.
        -->
        <customErrors mode="RemoteOnly" />

    </system.web>

</configuration>
```

Web.config files can also reside in various subdirectories of an application. Each web.config file governs the operation of pages within its directory and all lower subdirectories unless overridden. Entries made in a lower-level web.config file override those made in levels above them. Some users find this counterintuitive; some don't. The master file specifying the defaults for the entire ASP.NET system has the name machine.config and lives in the directory [system, e.g. WINNT]\Microsoft.NET\Framework\[version]. Entries made in web.config files in the root directories of an individual Web application override entries made in the master file. Entries made in web.config files in subdirectories of an application override those made in the root. This relationship is shown in Figure 3-14. An administrator can mark entries as non-overridable if so desired.

A setting made in a web.config file overrides the settings made in directories above it.

Figure 3-14 *The hierarchical nature of web.config files.*

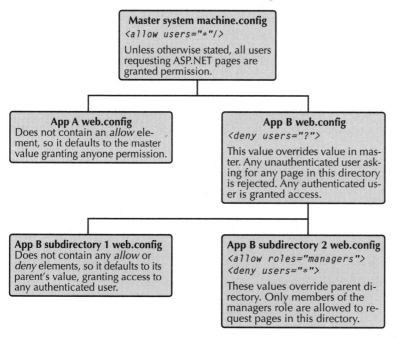

Not all sections of the web.config file are configurable on all levels of subdirectory. The *<sessionstate>* section, for example, may not appear below an application's root directory. You'll have to examine the details of individual sections to find out the granularity of each.

At the time of this writing, this configuration scheme is difficult
to use. You can edit the raw XML file using any editor, or Visual
Studio.NET provides a slightly better tool as shown in Figure 3-15.
But it still falls far below the ease of use of any other administrative tool in the Windows 2000 environment—the COM+ Explorer,
for example. The ASP.NET team acknowledges the need for a better tool but has decided that it needs to finish working on the feature set of the product itself before writing the administrative tools,
even if this causes the administrative tools to ship some time after
the product release. While I disagree (respectfully but strongly)
with this call, I can tell you that the problem is being worked on.
I've seen some of the prototypes that the Microsoft developers are
working on, and they're pretty cool. While major design choices
are still under discussion and no schedule has been announced, I
am now convinced that the ASP.NET team realizes that good administrative tools are critical to the product's success in the marketplace. I believe these tools will be shipped not too long after
the .NET Framework does. I guarantee that the product won't take
off until they do.

Figure 3-15 *Visual Studio.NET provides a crude tool for editing
configuration files.*

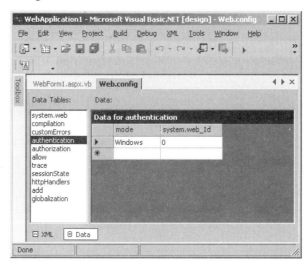

ASP.NET State Management

Web page requests are by default independent of each other. If I request page B from a server, the contents of page B don't know whether I have or haven't viewed page A a few minutes ago. This arrangement works well for simple read-only requests, such as the movie theater example I discussed in the opening paragraph of this chapter. It's easy to write a server that does this because you don't have to store any data from one page request to another.

Internet page requests from a single user didn't originally know about each other. Sometimes this is OK.

As Web interactions get more sophisticated, however, this design no longer meets your users' needs. What I did on page A *does* affect the content that page B should show. For example, I book a lot of air travel directly on airline Web sites because they offer extra frequent flyer miles. It's not acceptable to me to search for an outgoing flight, write it down on paper, search for a return flight, write it down as well, and then manually type both of these flight numbers into yet another page for purchasing my ticket. I want the airline's site to automatically remember my outgoing flight selection while I choose a return flight and then remember both of these while I buy the ticket.

Then again, as Web interactions get richer, sometimes it isn't.

Remembering data from one form to another was never a problem for a desktop application, which targeted a single user. The programmer could simply store input data in the program's internal memory without worrying about which user it belonged to, since only one person used the program at a time. But keeping track of a user's actions over multiple pages is much more difficult in a Web application, used by (you hope) many different people simultaneously. A Web programmer needs to keep my data separate from all the other users' so that their flights don't get mixed with mine (unless they're headed to Hawaii in February, in which case, hooray!). We call this *managing session state*, and the Web programmer needs some efficient, easy-to-program way of doing it.

A Web programmer often must maintain separate data for many users simultaneously.

Original ASP provided a simple mechanism for managing session state, which ASP.NET supports and extends. Every time a new user accesses an .ASPX page, ASP.NET creates an internal object called a *Session*. This object is a collection of data living on the server and tied to a particular active user. The Web programmer can store in the *Session* object any type of data he cares about. The *Session* object automatically remembers (placing a unique ID in a browser cookie or appending it to the URL) which user the data refers to, so the programmer doesn't have to write code to do that. For example, when I submit a form selecting a flight, the .ASPX page programmer can store that flight's information in the *Session* object. When I request the page to buy my ticket, the programmer reads the flight from my *Session* object. The .ASPX run time automatically knows who the user is (me), so the programmer's code automatically fetches my flights and not someone else's, as shown in Figure 3-16. The *Session* object can hold any number of strings for each user, but since they all use server memory, I advise you to limit the amount of data you store in session state to the minimum necessary.

Figure 3-16 *Managing session state.*

ASP.NET provides a set of data tied to a specific user. Called a *Session*, programmers can use this object to store data for a specific user.

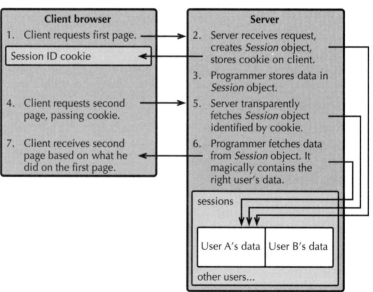

This feature is easy for programmers to use, and hence quite popular. Each .ASPX page contains a property named *Session* that provides access to the *Session* object for the current user. You store data in this object using a string key, and fetch it the same way. A sample of the code that does this is shown in Figure 3-17. You will also find this sample on this book's Web site. The pages will look like Figure 3-18.

Figure 3-17   *Code for session state management.*

```
' Code that stores data in session state.

Protected Sub Button1_Click(ByVal sender As System.Object, _
                            ByVal e As System.EventArgs) _
                            Handles Button1.Click

    ' Store current text string in session state.

    Session("DemoString") = TextBox1().Text

    ' Redirect user to page for viewing state.

    Response().Redirect("WebForm2.aspx")

End Sub


' Code that retrieves data from session state.

Protected Sub Page_Init(ByVal Sender As System.Object, _
                        ByVal e As System.EventArgs) _
                        Handles MyBase.Init
    'CODEGEN: This method call is required by the Web Form Designer.
    'Do not modify it using the code editor.
    InitializeComponent()

    ' Fetch string from session state. Show in label.

    Try
        Label2().Text = Session("DemoString").ToString

        ' If the named session state string does not exist, referencing
        ' it causes an exception. Handle it cleanly.

    Catch ex As Exception
        Label2().Text = "(session string is empty)"
    End Try

End Sub
```

ASP.NET provides a simple API for setting and getting session state variables.

Figure 3-18 *Session state management sample application.*

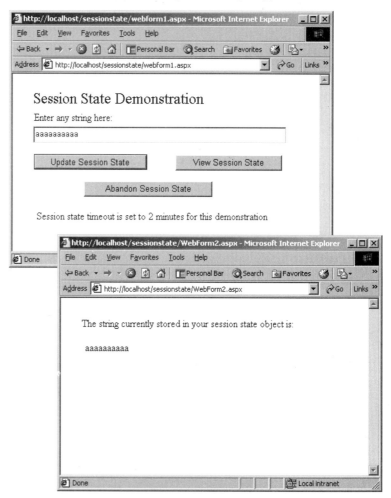

Obviously, if a server were to maintain a permanent session for every user that ever viewed even one page on it, you'd run out of memory very quickly. The session mechanism is designed to maintain state only for active users—those who are currently performing tasks that require the server to maintain state for them. ASP.NET automatically deletes a user's *Session* object, dumping its contents, after it has been idle for a configurable timeout interval. This interval is set in the *<sessionstate>* section of the web.config file, shown in Figure 3-19. You can also dump the session yourself by calling the method *Session.Abandon*.

<aside>
ASP.NET automatically deletes sessions after a configurable timeout interval.
</aside>

Figure 3-19 *Session state management entries in the web.config file.*

```
<sessionState
        mode="inproc"
        stateConnectionString="tcpip=127.0.0.1:42424"
        sqlConnectionString="data source=127.0.0.1;user id=sa;password="
        cookieless="false"
        timeout="2"
    />
```

While the session mechanism in original ASP was easy to use, it had a number of drawbacks that hampered its expansion to large-scale systems. First, it stored session state in the worker processes that actually ran page scripts and called code living in programmer-written custom objects. A badly behaved object could and often did crash this process, thereby killing the session state of every user it was currently serving, not just the one whose call caused the crash. ASP.NET fixes this problem by providing the ability to store session state in a separate process, one that runs as a system service (see Figure 3-20), so badly behaved user code can't kill it. This means that worker processes can come and go without losing their session state. It slows down the access to the session state somewhat, as applications now need to cross process boundaries to get to their session state, but most developers figure that's worth it for reliability. To turn this feature on, set the *mode* attribute in the web.config file to *stateserver* and ensure that the state server process is running on the server machine.

Session state can be stored in a separate process for robustness.

Figure 3-20   *ASP.NET session state process running as a system service.*

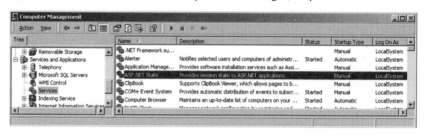

Session state can be easily stored on a different machine

Original ASP always stored session state on the server machine on which it was created. This architecture didn't scale well to a Web farm in which every request is potentially handled by a different server. ASP.NET allows each application to specify the machine on which it wants its session state to be stored. You do this by setting the *stateConnectionString* attribute in the web.config file. In this way, any machine that handles a subsequent call can access the session state stored by a previous call handled by a different machine. Obviously, you now incur the overhead of another network round-trip, so maybe you'd rather set up your load balancer to route subsequent requests to the same machine. You can swap out that machine by simply changing its name in the configuration files of all the clients.

You can also store session state in a SQL Server database.

You can also store session state in SQL Server for better management of large collections. You do this by setting the *mode* attribute to *sqlserver* and providing a SQL connection string in the *SqlConnectionstring* attribute. The current setup scripts create a temporary database for holding session state. This provides fast access because the data isn't written to the slow iron disk, but it also means that the session state won't survive a crash. If you want that durability and don't mind paying the performance penalty for it, you can change the database attributes yourself to use a permanent table.

ASP.NET also helps you manage application state, where an application represents a top-level IIS virtual directory and all of its subdirectories. Application-level state is stuff that changes from time to time, so you don't want to hard code it, but it applies to all users of the application and isn't tied to an individual user. An example of application state might be the current unadvertised special offer that every page would display. Each application contains one state object named *Application*, similar in use to the *Session* object, except that all accesses of the *Application* object operate on the same data regardless of the user on the other end.

ASP.NET also provides another state collection for data at an application level.

Security in ASP.NET

Security is vital to any type of distributed programming, and discussions of it are often highly charged with emotion. I will attempt to outline the problems that arise in this area and discuss how ASP.NET provides your Web application with prefabricated functionality that gives you the level of security you need without too much programming effort.

Security is vital to any distributed system.

The security requirements of a Web application are somewhat like those of a city hall. You have large numbers of people coming and going anonymously, accessing public areas such as the tourism office that dispenses maps. Because these areas aren't sensitive, you don't want to waste time and annoy users by subjecting them to strip searches. But other areas of the same city hall, such as the floor containing the mayor's office, are sensitive. You don't want to allow anyone in who can't prove their identity (authentication) and that they have business on the floor (authorization). And you might want to run them through a metal detector to make sure they can't hurt anybody.

Different areas of an application require different levels of security.

Authentication

The first problem in security is authentication—Who are you, and how do I know you really are that person? Authenticating a user usually takes the form of examining some sort of credential presented by the user, sometimes agreed upon directly between the two parties, such as a PIN or password; sometimes issued by a third party that both trust, such as a driver's license or passport. If the credentials are satisfactory to the server, the server knows who the user is and can use its internal logic to determine what actions she is allowed to perform. A user who is not authenticated is called an anonymous user. That doesn't necessarily mean that she can't have access to anything on the Web site. It means that she can have access only to the features that the designers have made available to anonymous users—perhaps checking an airline schedule but not redeeming a frequent flyer award.

Authentication has historically been the most difficult problem in security design. Most application designers don't want to deal with it because it's so important but so difficult to get right. You need a full-time team of very smart geeks who do nothing but eat, drink, and sleep security because that's what the bad guys have who are trying to crack your Web site and weasel free first-class upgrades (or worse). For example, you can't just send a password over the network, even if it's encrypted. If the network packet containing even an encrypted password doesn't somehow change unpredictably every time you submit it, a bad guy could record it and play it back. That's how I broke into the foreign exchange system of a certain bank whose name you would recognize—fortunately with the bank's permission—under a consulting contract to test their security. They were very proud of their password encryption algorithm, which I never even tried to crack, but it took me only 20 minutes with a packet sniffer to record a user ID/password packet and play it back to enter their server. Too bad I was charging them by the hour. Next time I'll vacation for a billable week before declaring success.

Because of the difficulty and importance of authentication, it's one of the first features that gets built into a (hopefully) secure operating system. ASP.NET supports three different mechanisms for authentication (four if you count "none"). They are shown in Table 3-2.

Fortunately, several different types of authentication come built into ASP.NET.

Table 3-2   ASP.NET authentication modes

Name	Description
None	No ASP.NET authentication services are used.
Windows	Standard Windows authentication is used from IIS.
Forms	ASP.NET requires all page request headers to contain a cookie issued by the server. Users attempting to access protected pages without a cookie are redirected to a log-in page that verifies credentials and issues a cookie.
Passport	Same idea as Forms, except that user ID info is held and cookies are issued by Microsoft's external Passport authentication service.

You need to think carefully about exactly where in your Web site authentication should take place. As with a city hall, you need to balance security versus ease of use. For example, a financial Web site will require authentication before viewing accounts or moving money, but the site probably wants to make its marketing literature and fund prospectuses available to the anonymous public. It is important to design your site so that secure features are secure, but you don't want this security to hamper your unsecure operations. I have a hard time thinking of anything more detrimental to sales than making a user set up and use an authenticated account before allowing him to see a sales pitch, although some sites do just that.

You need to think carefully about which of your site's resources require authentication for access and which don't.

WARNING: Unlike DCOM, which used its own wire format to support packet privacy, none of the authentication schemes available to ASP.NET provide for encryption of the data transmitted

Authentication in ASP.NET does not provide data encryption. You need to do that yourself.

from client to server. This problem doesn't come from ASP.NET itself, but from the common Web transport protocol HTTP. If your Web site provides data that you don't want on the front page of *USA Today*, you need to use the Secure Socket Layer (SSL) transport or provide some other mechanism for encrypting. Typically, you will do this only for the most sensitive operations because it is slower than nonsecure transports. For example, an airline Web site will probably use encrypted transport for the credit card purchase page but not for the flight search page.

Windows Authentication

Windows authentication works well on a Windows-only intranet.

ASP.NET supports what it calls *Windows-based authentication*, which basically means delegating the authentication process to IIS, the basic Web server infrastructure on which ASP.NET sits. IIS can be configured to pop up a dialog box on the user's browser and accept a user ID and password. These credentials must match a Windows user account on the domain to which the IIS host belongs. Alternatively, if the client is running Microsoft Internet Explorer 4 or higher on a Windows system and not connecting through a proxy, IIS can be configured to use the NTLM or Kerberos authentication systems built into Windows to automatically negotiate a user ID and password based on the user's current logged-in session.

Windows authentication works quite well for a Windows-only intranet over which you have full administrative control. For certain classes of installation—say, a large corporation—it's fantastic. Just turn it on and go. But it's much less useful on the wide-open Internet, where your server wants to be able to talk to any type of system, (say, a palmtop) using any type of access (say, not IE), and where you don't want to set up a Windows login account for every user.

Forms-Based, or Cookie, Authentication

Most designers of real-life Web applications will choose *forms-based authentication*, otherwise known as *cookie authentication*. The user initially sets up an account with a user ID and password. Some Web sites, such as most airline sites, allow you to do this over the Web through a page open to anonymous access. Other Web sites, such as most financial services companies, require a signed paper delivered via snail mail.

Forms-based authentication starts with a user ID and password.

When the user first requests a page from a secure Web site, he is directed to a form that asks for his ID and password. The Web server matches these against the values it has on file and allows access if they match. The server then provides the browser with a cookie that represents its successful log-in. Think of this cookie as the hand stamp you get at a bar when they check your ID and verify that you really are over 21 years old. It contains the user's identification in an encrypted form. The browser will automatically send this cookie in the request header section of every subsequent page request so that the server knows which authenticated user it comes from. This relay keeps you from having to enter a user ID and password on every form submittal or page request. Figure 3-21 illustrates this process.

Figure 3-21 *Forms-based authentication.*

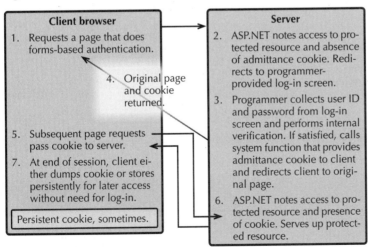

The server supplies the browser with a cookie, an admission ticket identifying the authenticated user.

When it supplies the cookie, the server specifies whether it is to be thrown away when the browser session ends or should be saved on the user's hard disk so that he won't have to log in next time. Financial Web sites often require the former in order to be ultra-protective against unauthorized use that could cost thousands of dollars. The latter, however, is obviously much more convenient for users. Most Web sites whose data isn't very sensitive, on-line periodicals such as the *Wall Street Journal* for example, often provide the user with the capability to choose it. A sample persistent cookie is shown in Figure 3-22.

Cookies may be temporary or persistent.

Figure 3-22   *Persistent cookie created by sample application.*

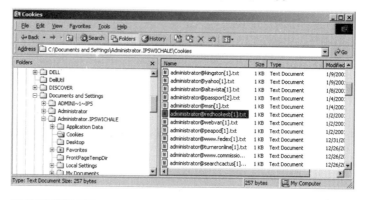

ASP.NET contains good support for forms-based authentication. A sample application is available on this book's web site and shown in Figure 3-23. You tell ASP.NET to use forms-based authentication by making an entry in the web.config file as shown in Figure 3-24. The *authorization* element tells ASP.NET to deny access to any unauthenticated users.

Figure 3-23 *Sample application for forms-based authentication.*

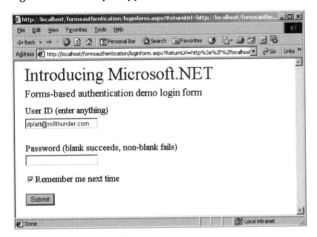

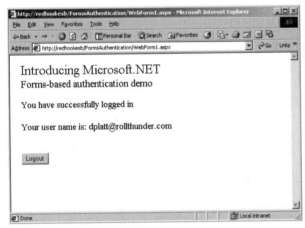

Figure 3-24 *Web.config file for forms-based authentication.*

```
<authentication mode = "Forms" >
    <forms name="IntroducingMicrosft.NET" loginUrl="loginform.aspx"/>
</authentication>

<authorization>
    <deny users="?"/>
</authorization>
```

This means that ASP.NET will require that any request for a page in that directory or its subdirectories must contain a cookie from the browser saying that you've authenticated the user and found him worthy. If the cookie is not present, as it won't be prior to your first log-in, ASP.NET directs the user to the page you have specified in the *loginUrl* attribute. You use this page to provide controls for the user to enter his ID and password. The page's handler contains whatever logic you need for checking that the user really is who he says he is. The sample code simply accepts a blank user password and rejects any that are nonblank. If the server accepts the incoming user, a simple function call (to *System.Web.Security.FormsAuthentication.RedirectFromLoginPage*) brings the user back to the page that he was trying to access when the authentication scheme shunted him to the log-in screen. The code is shown in Figure 3-25.

ASP.NET contains good prefabricated support for forms-based authentication.

Figure 3-25 *Code for forms-based authentication form.*

```
Public Sub Button1_Click(ByVal sender As Object, _
                         ByVal e As System.EventArgs)

    ' Accept a blank password. Call the function that sends a cookie
    ' to the client's browser and redirects the client to his original
    ' request page.

    If txt_Password.Text = "" Then
        System.Web.Security.FormsAuthentication.RedirectFromLoginPage( _
            txt_UserID.text, cb_RememberMe.Checked)

    ' Reject a non-blank password. Don't need to make any system calls,
    ' just refrain from making the one that would grant access.

    Else
        Label3.Text = "Invalid Credentials: Please try again"
    End If

End Sub
```

You can also set up ASP.NET to automatically perform forms-based authentication using user IDs and passwords stored in XML configuration files. This approach would probably work well for a small installation. Unfortunately, a demonstration is beyond the scope of this book, at least in this edition.

Passport Authentication

The third authentication alternative is Passport-based authentication. The forms-based scheme described in the previous section sounds fine, and it's a lot easier to write today than it used to be as the result of ASP.NET's prefabricated support. But it suffers from the fatal problem of unchecked proliferation. Every Web site with anything the least bit sensitive needs some sort of log-in security. For example, I use five different airline Web sites for booking all the travel I have to do, and because they take credit cards, every one of them requires authentication. It is a colossal pain in the ass to keep track of all the user names and passwords I use on these different sites. On one of them my name is "dplatt"; on another one that ID was taken when I signed up so I'm "daveplatt". I've tried using my e-mail address, which no one else ought to be using, and it occasionally works, but some sites won't accept the @ sign and others won't accept a string that long. For passwords, some use 4-character PINs for identification, others use a password of at least six (or sometimes eight) characters, and one insists that the password contain both letters and numbers. Many sites consider their data to be so sensitive (my frequent flyer record? get a life) that they won't allow a persistent cookie to remember my log-in credentials. The only way I can keep track of all my user names and passwords is to write them down and keep them near my computer, where any thief would look for them first. That's one way Nobel physicist Richard Feynman broke into classified safes and left goofy notes for fun while working on the atomic bomb

As Web sites proliferate, so do the user IDs and passwords that a user must remember. This is a growing menace to security of all data.

project at Los Alamos during World War II. (See his memoirs, *Surely You're Joking, Mr. Feynman,* for the other two ways. I guess Los Alamos has had this problem for a while.) As a client told me a decade ago, the greatest threat to security isn't the packet sniffer, it's the Post-It® note.

Microsoft Passport (*www.passport.com*) is an attempt to provide a universal one-step secure log-in procedure. It's very much like the forms-based authentication mechanism described in the preceding section, except that Microsoft's Passport Web servers handle the storing and verifying of user IDs and passwords. A user can go to the Passport Web site and create a passport, essentially a user ID and password stored on Microsoft's central server farm. When the user requests a page from a site that uses Passport authentication, that site looks for a Passport cookie in the request. If it doesn't find one, it redirects the request to Passport's own site, where the user enters her ID and password and receives a Passport cookie. Subsequent browser requests to any Passport-compliant site will use that cookie until the user logs out. The process is illustrated in Figure 3-26. A user can thus use the same user ID and password pair at any participating site. This scheme could greatly simplify the proliferation problem and make many users' lives easier, with a net gain in security.

Passport also allows a user to store personal information that he wants to easily provide to the Web sites that he visits. For example, a user's passport can contain snail mail addresses to allow Web sites to automate the procedures of filling out delivery forms; even credit card numbers for making purchases. The idea seems to be to make Amazon.com's fantastically successful (and patented) one-click ordering available to any willing site. You can see a Passport Express Purchase button on a few sites; Crutchfield.com or RadioShack.com are examples.

Figure 3-26 *Passport authentication.*

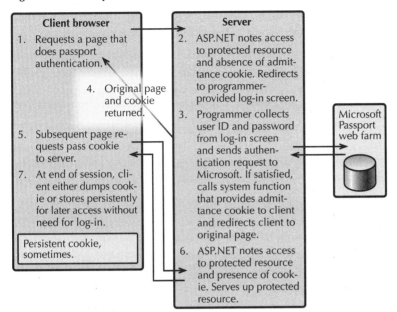

Client browser
1. Requests a page that does passport authentication.
4. Original page and cookie returned.
5. Subsequent page requests pass cookie to server.
7. At end of session, client either dumps cookie or stores persistently for later access without need for log-in.

Persistent cookie, sometimes.

Server
2. ASP.NET notes access to protected resource and absence of admittance cookie. Redirects to programmer-provided log-in screen.
3. Programmer collects user ID and password from log-in screen and sends authentication request to Microsoft. If satisfied, calls system function that provides admittance cookie to client and redirects client to original page.
6. ASP.NET notes access to protected resource and presence of cookie. Serves up protected resource.

Microsoft Passport web farm

Microsoft Passport offers a single ID and password pair for all participating sites.

Passport sounds like a good concept, but it remains to be seen how much market support it will attract. So far there's not that much. In addition to Microsoft's own Hotmail and MSN sites, Passport's own Web site currently (Jan 2001) lists only 65 sites, few of them large, that say they accept Passport authentication. And some of these (Victoria's Secret, for example) don't seem to have their implementations running yet. Part of the problem might be that Microsoft requires a licensing agreement to use Passport and charges fees for some of its services. Although the fees are currently waived for basic authentication, businesses might be worried about committing to such a scheme and seeing prices rise later. They might also be worried about outsourcing such an important piece of their online software presence. Since it's not under their control, how can they be sure it won't crash, or even slow

Passport can also contain information such as addresses and credit cards.

The future of Passport depends on acceptance by the business community.

below acceptable limits? How many would fear a repetition of January 23, 2001, when a boneheaded Microsoft technician made an incorrect DNS entry that blocked access to most Microsoft sites, including Passport, for almost a day? (I wonder if that technician had to use Notepad to edit a raw XML file, in which case the problem might have been avoided with a dedicated configuration tool.) And what about a falling out later? How could a Web company tell Microsoft to go to hell if Microsoft holds its login data?

Acceptance by businesses depends on acceptance by consumers, in a circular fashion.

The same problem applies on the consumer side. Will users find the convenience of Passport compelling enough to get one? It depends how many sites accept a passport, which in turn depends on how many customers have them. Since all 60 million Hotmail users automatically have passports, the base of Passport users isn't starting from zero. What about customers who hold a religious loathing for Microsoft? I don't think Larry Ellison will ever request a passport, nor will Janet Reno. Are these customers few enough that sites are willing to ignore them, or perhaps support Passport side-by-side with a non-Passport log-in?

The e-commerce features have a bigger customer acceptance problem.

The additional data that Passport can hold seems to me more problematic. Will users trust Microsoft with their credit card numbers in return for easier purchasing? I wouldn't. It's not so much Microsoft I distrust, after all I give them my credit card number everytime I need to buy a needless upgrade, but what about all the online vendors that read the passport? How do I know that Radio Shack won't look at my passport unless I click the purchase button? How do I know they won't read my snail mail address and start sending me their stupid flyers? "They've promised us they wouldn't" isn't exactly the platinum standard of privacy. Even if Microsoft really did make unwarranted reading of passport information impossible, how many consumers would believe it? While the universal log-in is a neat idea, I'll bet that the e-commerce features go nowhere. Spending my money's already easy enough; I don't need or even want it made any easier.

Passport is an interesting idea, and the market will determine its success or failure, as it should. I probably wouldn't choose it as my sole authentication mechanism today, but I'd give serious thought to offering it as an option. Anything that makes my site easier to use than my competitors' sites is a good thing. If you decide that you'd like to do Passport authentication, you'll find that the prefabricated support in ASP.NET makes it quite easy. You set the authentication mode to Passport in the web.config file. You will have to download the Passport SDK, sign a licensing agreement, and then write some simple code that delegates the authentication process to Passport.

ASP.NET includes pre-fabricated support for Passport authentication.

Authorization

Once the authentication process is complete, we know who the user is or know that the user is anonymous. We now need to decide whether the user should be allowed to see the page he is requesting. This is called *authorization*.

Once we've authenticated the user, we need to check whether the user is authorized to do what he's trying to do.

ASP.NET contains good support for controlling access to .ASPX pages. You can administratively limit access to pages by making entries in your application's web.config files, as shown in Figure 3-27.

You can administratively specify which users are allowed to view various pages by making entries in the web.config files for specific pages or directories.

Figure 3-27 *Authorization entries in a web.config file.*

```
<!-- Authorization

    This allows a user named Simba, and any users belonging to the
    role Doctors, to access pages in this directory (and any
    subdirectories that don't override this setting in their own
    web.config files).
-->

<authorization>
    <allow users="Simba" roles="Doctors" />
    <deny users="*" />
</authorization>
```

The *<authorization>* section contains *<allow>* and *<deny>* elements that respectively allow and deny[2] the specified users and members of the specified roles (groups of users) access to pages in the directories to which the web.config files apply. These elements can also accept a *verb* attribute (not shown) so that you can allow some users to view the page with a *get* operation but forbid them to post anything back to the server. Although web.config files apply to an entire directory (and its subdirectories unless overridden lower down), you can administratively restrict access to a single file by using the *<location>* element (not shown).

ASP.NET applies the administrative access rules in the order in which they appear.

When a user requests a page, ASP.NET applies the rules specified in the web.config file in the order in which they appear until it finds a rule that tells it whether to grant or deny the requesting user access to the requested page. If ASP.NET can't tell from the entries made in that file, it will look in the web.config file in that directory's parent and so on until it reaches the master ASP.NET machine.config file discussed previously. That file, by default, grants access to all requests. So if you don't want people to see a certain file, you'll have to explicitly put in a *<deny>* element. In the example shown in Figure 3-26, ASP.NET will first apply the *<allow>* element. If the user is named "Simba" or is a member of a role named "Doctors," access is granted and the checking process ends. If neither of these tests is true, ASP.NET applies the next rule, which says to deny access to everybody (the * character). ASP.NET will fail the request, and the checking process will end. In this way, only Doctors and Simba can view the pages of this subdirectory. Note that when using Windows authentication on a domain, you must prepend the domain name onto the role or user name in order for ASP.NET to recognize it, as shown in Figure 3-28.

---

2   Well, duh!

Figure 3-28 *Web.config file showing authorization entries for domain users using Windows authentication.*

```
<!-- Authorization

    This does the same thing as the previous example, except
    user ID and role names are prefixed with the domain name so as to
    work correctly with Windows authentication on a domain.
-->

<authorization>
    <allow users="REDHOOKESB0\Simba"/>
    <allow roles="REDHOOKESB0\Doctors"/>
    <deny users="*" />
</authorization>
```

Since it is likely that our Web site will be used by many anonymous users—those who have not been authenticated—we need a way of specifying what they are allowed to do. The question mark character (?) denotes anonymous users. You use it exactly like any other name or the '*' character. You can see an example in Figure 3-23, the web.config file used for forms-based authentication. It says that unauthenticated users aren't allowed to view pages in that directory, thereby forcing them to the login form to become authenticated.

> The '?' character allows you to set permissions for unauthenticated users.

ASP.NET allows you to authorize either individual users or entire roles. Most real-life installations perform little or no authorization on an individual user basis; it's almost always done on a group basis. For example, a hospital prescription application might allow physician's assistants to prescribe Tylenol, but only licensed doctors to prescribe controlled narcotics. These permissions will be set for each role, and individual users added to or removed from role membership as required.

> Most real-life authorization works with roles, which are groups of users.

ASP.NET automatically determines role membership when you use Windows authentication.

When you use Windows authentication, ASP.NET automatically recognizes a role as any standard Windows user group set up by the administrator. Every user assigned to that group is a member of the role. You don't have to program anything, recognition just automatically happens. When you use cookie or Passport authentication, however, the definition of a role becomes much more difficult. ASP.NET doesn't know how your user data is stored or what constitutes role membership in your application. You therefore have to write your own code and plug it into the ASP.NET environment so that it can call you to ask whether a user is a member of a specified role. Basically, you have to write a class that implements the *IPrincipal* interface, which includes the method *IsInRole*. In this method, you place whatever code you want for determining whether a specified user is a member of a specified role. (You could also try using the *GenericPrincipal* class, which allows you to plug in a simple array of strings giving a user's role membership.) You plug this class into ASP.NET in the *OnAuthenticate* method (expect a name change in later versions) in your application's global.asax file. ASP.NET will then call this class every time it needs to know whether a user is a member of a specified role. The code is shown in Figure 3-29. While this scheme isn't quite as bad to write as it sounds, I would have really liked to see a simple default mechanism for specifying role membership, with no need to write your own code unless you wanted something different. Since Microsoft did that for user IDs and passwords (see the end of the forms-based authentication section earlier in the chapter), they could easily add a role membership attribute to the user element and go from there.

You have to write your own code to determine role membership when you use cookie or Passport authentication.

Figure 3-29 *Code that handles role membership in forms-based or Passport authentication.*

```
Imports System
Imports System.Security
Imports System.Security.Principal


Public Class MyOwnRoleCheckerPrincipal : Implements IPrincipal

    Dim MyIdentity As IIdentity

    Public Sub New(ByRef id As IIdentity)
        MyIdentity = id
    End Sub

    Public Function IsInRole(ByVal role As String) As Boolean _
        Implements System.Security.Principal.IPrincipal.IsInRole

        If ( <role checking logic goes here> ) Then
            Return True
        Else
            Return False
        End If
    End Function

    <other methods>

End Class
```

Identity

The automatic authorization provided by ASP.NET is fine for controlling access to pages on your Web site. However, your Web pages usually represent the middle tier of a three-tier system, mediating access to a database behind it (the data tier). The middle tier performs business logic, such as determining whether the user

Your Web site is usually the middle tier of a three-tier system, mediating access to a data tier.

attempting to prescribe morphine is a licensed doctor. If this business logic is successful, the middle tier will communicate with the data tier to subtract morphine from the pharmacy inventory and to add another item to the patient's billing statement. If not, the middle tier will probably generate a fascinating game to keep the user occupied while it calls the police.

The security identity of the Web server process is important.

The back-end data tier almost certainly has its own security mechanisms. All commercial databases allow administrators to set access permissions of various granularity, specifying which users are allowed access to various databases and tables and which are not. Even the NTFS file system allows an administrator to specify which users or groups of users are allowed to perform which operations on which files and directories. These depend critically on what the data tier considers to be the identity of the user making the request for services.

The data tier usually trusts the middle tier to perform authorization.

The first, and probably the one that you'll wind up using, is called the *trusted user* model. In this model, the server process runs with a particular identity, say, PharmacyApp, known as the trusted user. The data tier is configured to allow this user to do anything in the database that it might need to in order to get its work done. For example, the trusted user identity used for the pharmacy application will have permission to make entries in the pharmacy inventory tables and the patient billing tables but probably not the patient census tables or the employee payroll records. The data tier trusts the middle tier server to have done all the authorization checking that needs to happen—for example, to have checked that the doctor's license is current so that it doesn't perform a second authorization. You trust your spouse to go through your wallet, so you don't bother asking what the money is for. This relationship is shown in Figure 3-30. You specify the identity of your server process via the *<identity>* element in your application's web.config file, as shown in Figure 3-31.

Figure 3-30 *Trusted user model of authorization.*

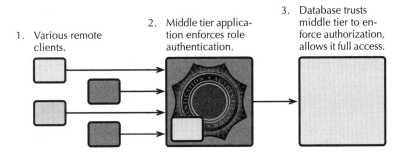

1. Various remote clients.
2. Middle tier application enforces role authentication.
3. Database trusts middle tier to enforce authorization, allows it full access.

Figure 3-31 *Web.config file specifying server process identity.*

```
<identity impersonate="false"
          userName="MyDomain\MyUsername"
          password="MyPassword" />
```

Your .ASPX page code can perform its own authorization via the intrinsic object named *User*. This object contains a method called *IsInRole*, which will tell you whether the user is a member of the administrative group that I've discussed previously. It is conceptually identical to the similar method seen in COM+. Usually that's all you need. If you want to go deeper and work with individual users, you can use the *Identity* property of the *User* object. This call returns an *IIdentity* interface, which tells you the authenticated user's name and the authentication mechanism used to verify that name. You write your own code that uses that information to decide whether the user is allowed to do what she's asking to do. I've provided a demonstration of this programmatic authorization as part of the Windows authentication sample shown previously. The sample authorization page is shown in Figure 3-32 and its code in Figure 3-33.

ASP.NET provides an object allowing your code to check user identity to perform programmatic authorization.

Figure 3-32 *Sample Web page showing trusted user authorization.*

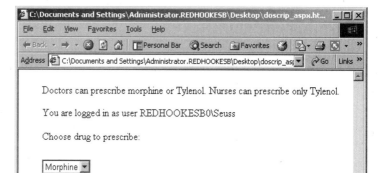

Figure 3-33 *Code showing trusted user authorization.*

```
Public Sub Button1_Click(ByVal sender As Object, _
                         ByVal e As System.EventArgs)

    Session("DrugName") = DropDownList1.SelectedItem.Text
    Session("Result") = "OK"

    ' If user is trying to prescribe morphine and isn't a member of
    ' the role "Doctors", then fail the request.

    If DropDownList1.SelectedItem.Text = "Morphine" Then
        If (User.IsInRole("Doctors") = False) Then
            Session("Result") = "BAD"
        End If
    End If

    Response.Redirect("ScripResult.aspx")
End Sub
```

Sometimes the trusted user model doesn't fit.

Not every database installation is comfortable with this approach. Many databases were designed and database administrators trained before three-tier programming became popular. Particularly with legacy systems, it often happens that the database layer contains security checks or audit trails that depend on the actual database entry being made under the network identity of the base client.

In this case, if you're using Windows authentication, you can fall back on the older *impersonation-delegation* model, as used by original ASP. In this model, the .ASPX page code takes on the identity of ("impersonates") the authenticated user (or uses a special identity designated for anonymous users). The page code then attempts to access the data-tier resource, and the resource itself, say, SQL Server, performs the authorization, checking to see whether the user is allowed access. This case is shown in Figure 3-34.

In this case, the Web server can impersonate the client, if you're using Windows authentication.

Figure 3-34 *Impersonation/delegation model of authorization.*

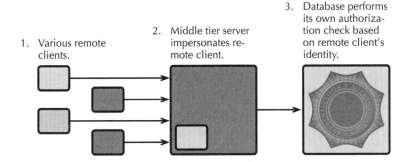

1. Various remote clients.

2. Middle tier server impersonates remote client.

3. Database performs its own authorization check based on remote client's identity.

While this approach may sound attractive, it is expensive in terms of performance. It requires two authentications instead of one: the first when ASP.NET authenticates the user prior to impersonating him, and the second when the database authenticates the server object's current impersonating identity. Furthermore, when authorization rejects a user, it does so rather late in the process. You've already gone down three tiers instead of two and made two network hops instead of one. It's better that you notice that you forgot your wallet when you arrive at the supermarket instead of after you've shopped and waited in the checkout line. It's better still to notice it when you first get in your car.

The Impersonation-Delegation model is expensive in terms of performance.

The Web server impersonates a client in one of two ways. Original ASP automatically impersonated the client every time a request was made. ASP.NET does not do this by default, but you can turn it on in the web.config file by setting the *impersonation* attribute shown in Figure 3-35 to *True.* Alternatively, you can

A Web server can impersonate a client programmatically, if using Windows authentication.

impersonate the client programmatically by calling the function *System.Security.Principal.WindowsIdentity.GetCurrent().Impersonate*. A Web page showing automatic impersonation is show in Figure 3-36.

Figure 3-35 *Web.config settings for automatic impersonation.*

```
<identity>
    <impersonation enable="true" />
</identity>
```

Figure 3-36 *Sample Web application demonstrating impersonation.*

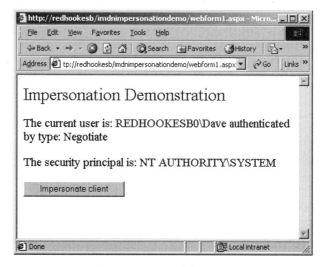

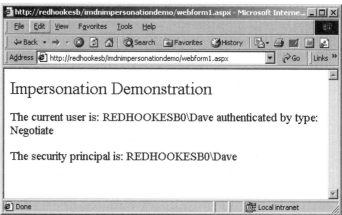

Process Management

One of the main features that we want in a Web server is unattended 24/7 operation. This level of service is a problem developers never really had to address in writing desktop applications. For example, memory leaks in a Solitaire game that runs for 5 minutes at a time (OK, 2 hours) probably won't waste enough memory to hurt anything. But if I kept the Solitaire game running for a year, redealing instead of closing it, any memory leaks would eventually exhaust the process's address space and cause a crash.

Robustness under load is a very important feature of a Web server.

That sort of robustness is very hard to develop, partly because it takes a long time to test. The only way to find out whether something runs for two weeks under load is to run it under load for two weeks. And when the crash does happen, it's often caused by a banana peel dropped days earlier, which is essentially impossible to find at the time of the crash.

It's also extremely difficult to develop. That figures.

I once (12 years ago) worked on an application that ran in a major bank. It was a DOS-based system (remember DOS?) that would usually run all day, but it just couldn't run for a week without crashing and we couldn't wring it out so that it could. I had the bright idea of putting a watchdog timer card into the machine that our software would periodically reset while it ran. If the timer ever actually expired without being reset, it would automatically reboot the system, sort of a "dead-geek" switch. The bank balked at installing such a god-awful kludge (we probably shouldn't have told them; we probably should have just done it and smiled) and instead agreed to have the administrator reboot the system every night.

Most software needs periodic restarting.

Original ASP kept a user process running indefinitely. Any bugs or memory leaks in any of the user code would accumulate and eventually cause crashes. ASP.NET recognizes that user code probably isn't going to be perfect. It therefore allows an administrator to configure the server to periodically shut down and restart worker processes.

ASP.NET supports process recycling to continue working robustly in the face of imperfect user code.

Configure process recycling using the *<processModel>* element of the machine-level machine.config file, as shown in Figure 3-37. I wish Microsoft had allowed process model configuration on a per-application basis, but they haven't at the time of this writing. You can tell ASP.NET to shut down your worker process and launch a new one after a specified amount of time (*timeout* attribute), a specified number of page requests (*requestLimit* attribute), or if the percentage of system memory it consumes grows too large (*memoryLimit* attribute). While not removing the need to make your code as robust as possible, this will allow you to run with a few memory leaks without rebooting the server every day or two. You can see that the process model contains other configurable capabilities as well.

You configure process recycling in the machine.config file.

Figure 3-37 *Machine.config file showing process recycling settings.*

```
<processModel
        enable="true"
        timeout="infinite"
        idleTimeout="infinite"
        shutdownTimeout="0:00:05"
        requestLimit="infinite"
        requestQueueLimit="5000"
        memoryLimit="80"
        webGarden="false"
        cpuMask="0xffffffff"
        userName=""
        password=""
        logLevel="errors"
        clientConnectedCheck="0:00:05"
        />
```

Chapter Four

.NET Web Services

Now, a' together, hear them lift their lesson—theirs an' mine:
"Law, Order, Duty an' Restraint, Obedience, Discipline!"
Mill, forge an' try-pit taught them that when roarin' they arose,
An' whiles I wonder if a soul was gied them wi' the blows.

> —Rudyard Kipling, writing on the mental toughness needed to
> work with high technology, "McAndrew's Hymn," 1894.

Problem Background

The primary user interaction model described so far in this book hasn't changed since the Web was created at CERN in Geneva for browsing boring physics reports. A human (or, in a famous cartoon, a dog) uses an all-purpose browser program to request a page from a server, the server decodes the request and supplies the page, the browser renders it for human viewing, and the human attempts to stay awake long enough to read it. Improved content (sports scores, pornography, Weird Al Yankovic music videos[1]) has largely solved the problem with boredom, but the final consumer of the requested data is still a human rather than a computer program.

The current structure of the Internet is designed to render pages for humans to read, not to provide data for client programs to process.

The great thing about the Internet, though, is that it's everywhere. Every intelligent device on the planet is connected to it, or soon will be. Users could reap great benefits if Web servers could

---

1. See his hilarious spoof of *Star Wars* at *www.sagabegins.com*

We could reap enormous benefits if dedicated client programs could use, request, and understand data from the Internet as easily as humans can.

provide data to programs running on all these devices as easily as they do pages for humans to look at. For example, developers could greatly enhance the user experience by writing an excellent, dedicated user interface that runs on a client machine rather than relying on a mediocre browser interface provided by the server. Think how much easier it is to process e-mail in Microsoft Outlook's dedicated user interface than it is in Hotmail's generic browser-based interface. (Of course, we could also screw up this opportunity by writing stupid UIs—death to the dancing paper clip!) The development of dedicated UIs would also improve server performance by moving the formatting of presentations to the client machine, having 1000 clients doing their own formatting instead of one server doing it for 1000 clients. Providing data from the Internet to a range of devices would also allow programs that don't have any user interface, such as a bank auditing program, to use the ubiquitous connectivity of the Internet without having to divide their program logic into page requests. Likewise, we'd allow the forthcoming generation of non-PC Internet devices, such as a telephone that uses the Internet instead of standard phone lines, to do the same thing.

Dedicating hardware and software to specific tasks makes them easier to use than a single generic device for everything.

The situation today, with Internet access primarily available through a generic browser program, is similar to the early part of the twentieth century, when electricity first started arriving in American households. Then, electric motors weren't usually built into household appliances. Sears, for example, sold a stand-alone electric motor (for $8.75) that you could connect to different appliances, such as your sewing machine, mixer, or fan.[2] This situation was difficult because you had to connect and configure the motor before you could use any appliance. You could probably afford only one motor, so you had to choose between sewing and fanning if your clothes needed mending on a hot day. And since the motor had to run with all kinds of different appliances, it didn't serve any of them particularly well. As motors got smaller and cheaper,

---

2. You can see a picture of this Sears catalog offering on page 50 of *The Invisible Computer*, by Donald Norman (MIT Press, 1999)

they were built into individual appliances, to the point that today it's difficult to buy a toothbrush or a carving knife that doesn't contain at least one. Modern appliances are easy to use because the motor and its infrastructure (power supply, linkages, and so on) are optimized for each specific task and hidden from you. You don't think about them; you just turn your appliance on and use its dedicated human interface.

The same sort of seismic shift is just now beginning in Internet programming. Just as motors got built into appliances, so Internet access will soon be built directly into every program anyone ever writes. You won't use a generic browser except when you feel like browsing generically. Instead, you will use dedicated programs that are optimized for accomplishing specific tasks. You won't think about the program's Internet access, as you don't really think about the motors in your appliances (except when they break, and the same will apply to dedicated Internet access programs). An early example of this type of program is Napster, which allows you to search the hard drives of thousands of participating users for music files that meet specified criteria, and then download the ones you like. A screen shot of this program, showing a search for songs freely and publicly released on the Internet by the artists, is shown in Figure 4-1. The dedicated user interface of a multiplayer game is another example of hidden Internet access. And the latest edition of Microsoft Money does a good job of seamlessly blending Web (current stock quotes, latest balances) and desktop content (financial plans you create locally).

Easy programmatic Web access would mean that developers could compose their applications from services available on the Web, as they now compose applications from prebuilt components available on their local PCs. The designer of a word processor, which people would consider strictly a desktop application, might not provide a spelling checker with the application or might supply only a rudimentary one. For more sophisticated spelling or definition services, the word processor could use the online edition of the *Oxford English Dictionary*, whose Web site, *oed.com*,

Application designers will compose their applications from services available on the Web, as they compose them today from prebuilt components on a user's machine.

modestly admits that it is "the most authoritative and comprehensive dictionary of English in the world."[3] This site charges a subscription fee and is currently available only to humans with generic browsers. If the OED provided seamless access to programs, they'd probably sell a lot more subscriptions. Maybe the word processor vendor could get a cut of the subscription fee. If they were really smart, they'd provide a seamless free trial for a few months so you got dependent on it and then take it away if you didn't start paying.

Dedicated Internet access needs to be "baked in" to every program, not just available through a generic browser.

Figure 4-1 *User interface of Napster, an application containing dedicated Internet access.*

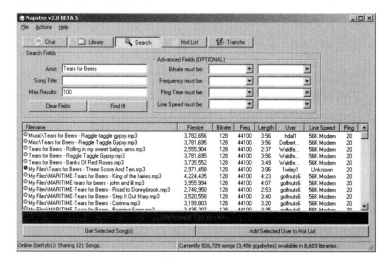

Most existing communication technologies only work with other instances of themselves.

To develop programs of this type, programmers need to be able to quickly and easily (which in turn means cheaply) write code that

---

3. I am currently trying to get the OED to accept a word that I coined in my Byte.com column of August 23, 1999. The word is MINFU, patterned after the military acronyms SNAFU and FUBAR, which have crossed into general usage. In polite company, MINFU stands for MIcrosoft Nomenclature Foul-Up, and it happens a lot. For example, referring to in-place activation of an embedded object as "visual editing" (to distinguish it from tactile editing, I guess, or olfactory editing) is a MINFU. The whole COM-OLE-COM-ActiveX-COM nomenclature debacle was and to this day remains a giant MINFU. When I wrote to the OED, they politely said, in part, "…*we will be looking for more general currency before we could consider including it in the OED.*" So far, I've gotten a couple of authors to use it, most notably David Chappell. I hope you'll all use it in your writing and send me a link to it, which I'll forward to the OED. You don't have to credit me, just use it. If I can get it into the Microsoft Press

style guide, I'll have it made.

communicates with other programs over the Internet. The idea isn't new; any number of techniques exist for this type of communication, such as RPC, DCOM, and MSMQ. Each of these techniques is cool in itself, and they all seemed like good ideas two or three years ago. However, they all share the fatal short coming that they only work from one similar system to another—MSMQ talks only to MSMQ, a DCOM client only to a DCOM server, and so on.

What we really need is universal programmatic access to the Internet—some way for a program on one box to call a function on any other box written by anyone. This access has to be independent not only of the operating system but also of the program's internal implementations. (C++ or Basic? Which vendor? Which version? We can barely solve this problem on a single desktop.) And it has to be easy to use, or no one will be able to afford the programming time to take advantage of it.

> We need universal, program-to-program, function-based communication over the existing Internet pathway.

Solution Architecture

The problem of universal programmatic access to the Internet is similar to the problem faced by designers of the international air traffic control system. A randomly changing set of heterogeneous nodes (different types of aircraft) need to talk to fixed servers (control towers) and each other. Their internal programming (the flight crews' thoughts) works in all kinds of different, incompatible languages (Thai, Norwegian, Californian). Communication between the flight crews, aircraft, and control towers has to work right or terrible things happen, such as on March 3, 1977, at Tenerife, when two 747s collided during takeoff because of misunderstood tower communications and 335 people died.

> International air traffic control faces a problem similar to universal Internet access.

Solving the problem requires agreement among all parties operating aircraft. Given the size (all aircraft operators in the world) and heterogeneity (rich and poor passenger airlines, cargo carriers, general aviation, military, smugglers, and so on) of this group, the only approach that stands any chance of working is to standardize

> The air traffic control problem was solved by agreeing on a lowest common denominator, the English language.

on the lowest common denominator in two critical areas. First, the mechanism for physically transmitting information from one party to another. Aircraft use VHF radios on designated frequencies. Second, air traffic control requires a standardized way of encoding the information transmitted. By international agreement, all pilots and control towers are required to use only English, even Air France landing at Charles de Gaulle International Airport in Paris (which annoys the heck out of them).

Like the solution for the air traffic control problem, the only way to deal with the enormous numbers of heterogeneous entities on the Internet is to use the lowest common denominator. When we decide how to transfer bytes from one box to another, we need to use something that every box on the Internet has, analogous to the VHF radio that every aircraft carries. The most common Internet transfer protocol is HTTP (Hypertext Transfer Protocol), which is used today by essentially all Web browsers to fetch the pages they display. We also need a lowest common denominator for encoding the information that we transfer with HTTP. As air traffic control uses English, our universal scheme will use XML (Extensible Markup Language) for encoding the data sent from one party to another.

The lowest common denominator on the Internet is HTTP and XML.

Microsoft put these ideas together and came up with the concept of *Web Services*. A Web Service is a seamless way for objects on a server to accept incoming requests from clients using the Internet's lowest common denominator of HTTP/XML. To create a Web Service you don't have to learn a new way to program. You simply write a .NET object as if it were being accessed directly by local clients, mark it with an attribute that says you want it to be available to Web clients, and ASP.NET does the rest. ASP.NET automatically hooks up a prefabricated infrastructure that accepts incoming requests through HTTP and maps them to calls on your object, as shown in Figure 4-2. When you roll your objects into a Web Service, they can work with anyone on the Web that speaks HTTP and XML, which should be everybody in the universe, no matter what type of operating system and run-time environment they're running in. You don't have to write the infrastructure that deals with Web communication; the .NET Framework provides it for you.

A Web Service seamlessly connects your .NET objects to incoming HTTP requests.

Figure 4-2 *Server-side view of ASP.NET Web Services*

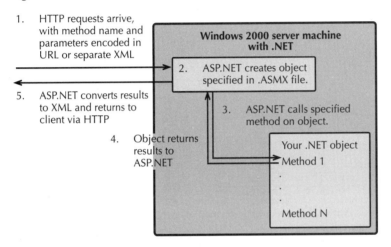

On the client side, .NET provides proxy classes that allow easy, function-based access to the Web Services provided by any server that accepts HTTP requests, as shown in Figure 4-3. A developer tool reads the description of the Web Service and generates a proxy class containing functions in whatever language you use to develop the client. When your client calls one of these functions, the proxy class creates an HTTP request and sends it to the server. When the response comes back from the server, the proxy class parses the results and returns them from the function. This allows your function-based client to seamlessly interact with any Web server that speaks HTTP and XML, which, again, should be everybody.

.NET also provides
proxy classes that make
it easy to write a Web
Service client by hiding
the details of Internet
communications.

Figure 4-3 *Client-side view of ASP.NET Web Services*

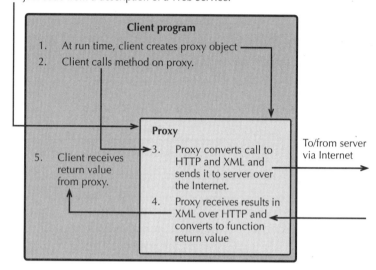

0. At programming time, a developer generates proxy
   object code from a description of a Web Service.

Client program

1. At run time, client creates proxy object
2. Client calls method on proxy.

Proxy

3. Proxy converts call to HTTP and XML and sends it to server over the Internet.

5. Client receives return value from proxy.

4. Proxy receives results in XML over HTTP and converts to function return value

To/from server via Internet

Simplest Example: Writing a Web Service

A Web Service example begins here.

As I always do when trying to learn or explain a new piece of technology, I've written the simplest sample program that I could think of to demonstrate Web Services. The program exposes a single method, called *GetTime*, that provides the current time on the server machine in the form of a string, either with or without the seconds digits. You can download the sample code for this service from this book's web site (*www.understandingmicrosoft. net*) and follow along with this description.

You don't need Visual Studio to write a Web Service; I wrote this one in Notepad.

I wrote this Web Service in the form of an ASP.NET page. I first installed the .NET SDK, a free download. I then used the normal Windows 2000 Internet Information Services (IIS) administrative tools to set up a virtual directory pointing to the folder in which I would do my Web Service file development. Then I wrote my ASP.NET code in a file named TimeService.asmx on my server. You don't need Visual Studio for this; in fact, I did the whole thing in Notepad. The program is shown in Figure 4-4.

Figure 4-4 *A basic Web Service.*

```
<%@ WebService Language="VB" Class="TimeService"%>

' The previous header line tells ASP.NET that this file contains
' a Web Service written in the Visual Basic language
' and that the name of the class providing that service
' is TimeService.

' Import the namespaces (think of them as references)
' required for a Web Service.

Imports System
Imports System.Web.Services


' Declare a new class for our new service. It must inherit
' from the system-provided base class WebService.

Public Class TimeService : Inherits WebService


' Place our functions in the class.
' Mark them as WebMethods.

Public Function <WebMethod()> GetTime (ShowSeconds as Boolean) _
    As String

    ' Perform the business logic of our function.
    ' Find current time, format as requested, and
    ' return the string.

    Dim dt As DateTime

    If (ShowSeconds = True) Then
        GetTime = dt.Now.ToLongTimeString
    Else
        GetTime = dt.Now.ToShortTimeString
    End If

End Function

End Class
```

While this program is quite simple, it contains a few constructs
that are probably new to you, so let's go over it section by section.

The program starts with the standard ASP.NET salutation, <%@ %>. In it we have the directive *WebService,* which tells ASP.NET that the code on the page should be exposed as a Web Service. The *Language* attribute tells ASP which language compiler to use for the code on the page. I've used Visual Basic because it's familiar to the greatest number of my readers. ASP.NET will use Visual Basic.NET to compile the code. You don't have to install Visual Studio; all the language compilers come with the .NET SDK. The *Class* attribute tells ASP.NET which object class to activate for incoming requests addressed to this service.

Your ASP.NET page specifies which .NET object class to use for the Web Service.

The rest of the page contains the code that implements the class. I used the *Imports* directive, a new feature of Visual Basic.NET, which tells the compiler to "import the namespaces." *Namespace* is a fancy way to refer to the description of a set of prefabricated functionality. It is conceptually identical to a reference in your Visual Basic 6 projects. Since ASP.NET will compile this example's code "just-in-time" when a request arrives from a client, I don't have a project in which to set these references. I have to explicitly add them to the code. The names following *Imports* tell the engine which sets of functionality to include the references for. In this case, *System* and *System.Web.Services* are the ones containing the prefabricated plumbing used in Web Services. Stop me if I get too technical.

ASP.NET will automatically compile your Visual Basic code the first time a request comes in for it.

The next line defines the name of our class. You've seen and written many classes in Visual Basic, and this one is very similar. My program uses a new keyword at the end of the line that reads *Public Class TimeService : Inherits WebService.* One of the main enhancements to Visual Basic.NET is its support for an object-oriented programming technique called *inheritance,* which I described in Chapter 2 and which you will grow to like. When I say that my new *TimeService* class inherits from the *WebService* class, I am telling the compiler to take all the code from the system-provided class named *WebService* (known as the *base class*) and include it in the *TimeService* class (known as the *derived class*). Think of inheritance as cutting and pasting without actually moving

Visual Basic now supports inheritance, which allows you to easily access prefabricated system features.

anything. In fact, deranged C++ and Java geeks often refer to physically cutting and pasting code as "editor inheritance." The *WebService* class is provided by the new .NET run-time library, just as many Visual Basic 6 objects were provided by the operating system. This class contains all the prefabricated plumbing required to handle the incoming HTTP requests and route them to the proper methods on your object.

Students often ask me what the difference is between importing the namespace and declaring inheritance; that is, the difference between the *Imports* and *Inherits* keywords. *Imports* brings in only the description of a set of functionality; it doesn't actually make use of it. As I said before, it's like setting a reference. *Inherits* actually takes part of the code referred to in the description and uses it. It's like *Dim As* on steroids.

Now that we've defined our class, we need to define the methods and functions of the class. Again, doing this is very similar to the way you do this in Visual Basic 6, with one new twist: you have to add the new attribute *<WebMethod( )>* to every method that you want exposed to Web clients. This attribute tells ASP.NET that the method in which it appears is to be exposed to clients as a Web Service. You've seen plenty of attribute-like elements in Visual Basic 6, such as *Public*, *Private*, and *Const*. Visual Basic.NET and the .NET Framework use many more of them, hence the new syntax for specifying them. Just as your class can contain public and private methods, it can contain some methods that are exposed to Web clients and others that are not.

You tell ASP.NET to expose your method as a Web Service by adding an attribute to the code.

Finally, we get down to the internals of our method. The handling of times might be a little new to you; it was to me. Don't worry about it today; it's just how Visual Basic.NET deals with dates and times.

You write your business logic in Visual Basic classes, pretty much as you've always done.

Now let's access our Web Service from a client. ASP.NET contains good prefabricated support for this as well. If you fire up Internet Explorer 5.5 and request the ASP.NET page we just wrote, you will see the page shown in Figure 4-5.

Figure 4-5 *Default screen generated by ASP.NET when you request the Web Service base page*

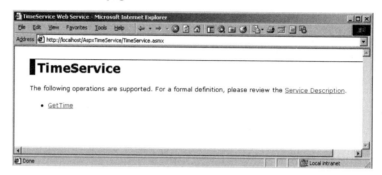

ASP.NET detects the access to the Web Service page itself (as opposed to one of the methods within the service) and responds with a page showing the list of functions supported by the service—in this case, only *GetTime*. If you click on the name of the function, ASP.NET will respond with a page that provides a test capability for this method, as shown in Figure 4-6. Enter TRUE or FALSE to tell *GetTime* whether to show the seconds digits , click Invoke, and the test page will call the specified method and return the results, as shown in Figure 4-7. You can see in the Address box that the parameters are passed in the URL and the results returned as XML. Also note that you must open the page in a way that goes through IIS, typing in a URL such as *http://localhost/[your virtual directory name]/TimeService.asmx*. If you simply double-click the page in Internet Explorer's view of your hard disk, you'll bypass IIS and ASP.NET and simply receive the text of the .ASMX page, which isn't what you're looking for.

The Web Service is as easy to administer and deploy as other .NET objects.

The convenient logistical and deployment features of .NET objects, described in Chapter 2, apply to my Web Service as well. For example, ASP.NET does not need registry entries to locate my object as COM did; instead, the URL specifies the location of my object. Updating the code is quite easy; I just copy the new file over the old one. (Try this with the sample code on your local machine.) It isn't locked as a COM server would be. I don't even have to restart my IIS server to make it notice the new file. It automatically detects the fact that the file has changed, compiles it just-in-time if necessary, and uses the new version for future object requests.

Figure 4-6 *ASP.NET responds with a page like this.*

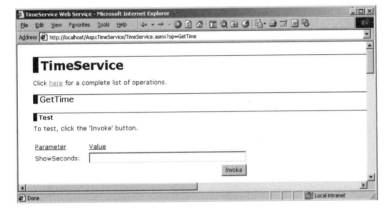

Figure 4-7 *Results returned by the Web Service*

ASP.NET automatically provides a simple browser-based client for testing your Web Service.

That's all I had to do to write my Web Service. It took only 13 lines, counting *Else* and *End If*. How much easier does it get?

This example demonstrated a lot of very powerful stuff that's quite easy to use.

Self-Description of Web Services: The WSDL File

For programmers to develop client applications that use our Web Service, we need to provide a description of what our service does and what programmers have to say to the service to get to do it. For example, a client of our Web Service would like to know the

Web Services need to provide a description of their functionality to interested clients.

methods the service exposes, the parameters they require, and the protocols they support—information conceptually similar to the type library that a standard COM component would carry. The problem with type libraries, however, is that they are Microsoft COM specific, and we want non-Microsoft systems to be able to become clients of our Web Service. We also want to be able to write descriptions of non-Microsoft services running on non-Microsoft systems so that our Microsoft-built client applications can use those services. What we need is a universal approach, not restricted to the Microsoft world, of describing a service. (Did you ever think you'd read these words in a Microsoft book? Me neither. Different world today.) And we need this approach to be machine-readable so that intelligent development environments can make use of it (again, like type libraries).

The description of a Web Service is provided in the form of a WSDL file. The .NET infrastructure can generate this description from your code.

The ASP.NET infrastructure can generate just such a description by examining the metadata (see Chapter 2) in the code that implements the service. The description is stored in an XML file that uses a vocabulary called WSDL (Web Service Descriptor Language).[4] The WSDL file for a Web Service is sometimes known as its *contract* because it lists the things that the service is capable of doing and tells you how to ask for them. You obtain the WSDL file from ASP.NET by requesting the .ASMX file with the characters *?WSDL* attached to the URL. For example, on my local machine, I obtained the file for my sample Web Service by requesting the URL *http://localhost/AspxTimeService/TimeService.asmx?WSDL*. That's what the Service Description link on the page shown in Figure 4-5 does.

---

4. You will note that many of the acronyms used in .NET aren't the TLAs (Three-Letter Acronyms; TLA itself is a TLA) you're used to seeing in most computing projects. That's because only 17,576 unique TLAs exist, and Microsoft ran out of them halfway through the project. I foresaw this problem two years ago and offered the solution of folding TLAs into CCTs (Clever Compound TLAs; CCT itself is a CCT). While the XML world seems to have adopted this idea (for example, XSL, XML Stylesheet Language, or SAX, Simple API for XML, a semisaturated CCT), Microsoft seems to have spurned it, opting instead to increase the word length to produce acronyms such as SOAP, WSDL, and UDDI. These nomenclature objects haven't been named yet, so I hereby declare them to be FLAPs, which stands for Four-Letter Acronym Packages. And, naturally, FLAP itself is a FLAP.

When you wrote COM components in Visual Basic 6 and Visual C++ 6, sometimes you wrote the component first and then wrote a type library to describe it. Other times you started with a type library describing an interface and wrote code that implemented it. WSDL can work in both of these ways as well. You can write the code first, as I've done in this sample, in which case ASP.NET will generate a WSDL file for interested clients. Alternatively, I could have written the WSDL file first, or gotten it from a third party, describing what the service should do, and then use the SDK utility program Wsdl.exe to generate a template file that implements the service that the WSDL file describes. (This approach is similar to using the *Implements* keyword in Visual Basic 6.)

Alternatively, you can write the description first and generate the code from it.

The WSDL file is somewhat complex, so I've extracted just one portion, shown in Figure 4-8, to illustrate the sorts of things that it contains. The *<service>* element contains a *<port>* element for each protocol that can be used to access the Web Service. In this case, you can see that the choices are HTTP GET, HTTP POST, and SOAP, which is an HTTP/XML hybrid. Each of the *<port>* elements in turn contains information referring to other elements in the document (which I don't show) that describe how each protocol requires its input request to be formatted and how it will format its output data.

A sample excerpt of a WSDL file is shown here.

Figure 4-8 *An excerpt from a WSDL file.*

```
<service name="TimeService">
  <port name="TimeServiceSoap" binding="s0:TimeServiceSoap">
    <soap:address
        location="http://localhost/AspxTimeService/TimeService.asmx" />
  </port>
  <port name="TimeServiceHttpGet" binding="s0:TimeServiceHttpGet">
    <http:address
        location="http://localhost/AspxTimeService/TimeService.asmx" />
  </port>
  <port name="TimeServiceHttpPost" binding="s0:TimeServiceHttpPost">
    <http:address
        location="http://localhost/AspxTimeService/TimeService.asmx" />
  </port>
```

Various development
tools read and interpret
WSDL for you.

`</service>`

Just as you usually interact with a type library by means of an interpretive viewer instead of picking apart its binary constituents, you will probably not deal with a raw WSDL file unless you are writing a programming tool that digests them. Instead, you will use WSDL files through interpretive tools, such as the test page provided by ASP.NET. In addition to the testing capacity shown previously in Figure 4-6, the same page interprets the WSDL file to show you the protocols it supports and the manner in which you must employ them in order to access the service. The screen shot in Figure 4-9 shows the portion of the page describing how to access our time service through the HTTP GET protocol.

Figure 4-9 *Client program accessing our Web Service using HTTP GET.*

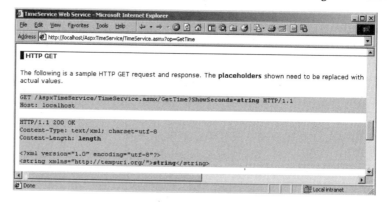

Writing Web Service Clients

I found writing a client as easy as writing the service itself. The ASP.NET listener that funnels incoming requests to Web Service objects accepts three different ways of packaging the incoming request. These are HTTP GET, HTTP POST, and SOAP. This is conceptually similar to an aircraft control tower speaking three dialects of English, say American, British, and Strine (Australian). The first two approaches are present primarily for backward compatibility, as essentially all code on the Web today uses one or the other of them. New development projects, however, will probably find it easier to use SOAP, particularly when you see the prefabricated support for this protocol that Visual Studio.NET provides. I'll look at each of these request mechanisms to examine how we would write a client that uses them.

Case 1: HTTP GET

My Web Service will accept a request through a simple HTTP GET request with the *ShowSeconds* parameter in the URL string. We saw the WSDL file describing our Web Service's support for this protocol in the previous section. A sample Web page providing access to this request is shown in Figure 4-10; the page is also available in this chapter's sample code. When the request reaches the server, ASP.NET parses the parameters from the URL string, creates the *TimeService* object, and calls the *GetTime* method. ASP.NET takes the return value of this method, formats it into XML, and returns the XML to the client. The return screen will look like Figure 4-7, shown previously.

The Web Service will accept a call via HTTP GET.

Figure 4-10   *Web page that accesses the example Web Service*

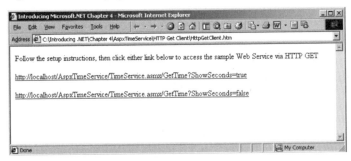

Case 2: HTTP Post

The Web Service will also accept an incoming call through an HTTP POST request. I examined the interpreted WSDL file referred to earlier to see exactly how I had to package my POST request to get the Web Service to recognize and respond to it. I then used Microsoft FrontPage 2000 to write a form that did the required things. A screen shot is shown in Figure 4-11, and the HTML code in Figure 4-12. (The file is provided with this chapter's sample code on the book's Web site.) When the request reaches the server, ASP.NET creates the *TimeService* object, pulls the parameters from the form's controls, and calls the *GetTime* method. It takes the return value of this method, formats it into XML, and returns the XML to the client.

Figure 4-11   *Client form that accesses the Web Service*

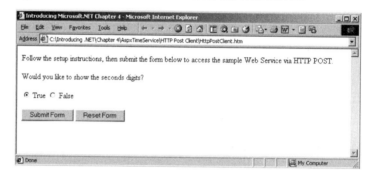

The Web Service will accept a call via HTTP POST.

Figure 4-12   *HTML for the client form*

```
<form METHOD="POST"
    ACTION="http://localhost/aspxtimeservice/timeservice.asmx/GetTime">
    <p>Would you like to show the seconds digits?</p>
    <blockquote><p>
        <input TYPE="RADIO" NAME="ShowSeconds" VALUE="True" CHECKED>
            True
        <input TYPE="RADIO" NAME="ShowSeconds" VALUE="False">
            False<br>
    </p></blockquote>
    <input TYPE="SUBMIT" VALUE="Submit Form">
    <input TYPE="RESET" VALUE="Reset Form">
</form>
```

Case 3: Raw SOAP

The Web Service will accept an incoming call request by means of an HTTP POST request that has all of its information encoded in a SOAP packet. No, not the stuff you wash with. SOAP, which stands for Simple Object Access Protocol, is an XML vocabulary that describes function calls and their parameters. Because of its richness and flexibility, and because of the built-in support for

SOAP in Visual Studio.NET, I expect that the developers of most new Web Service clients will choose SOAP rather than the HTTP GET or HTTP POST operations I've just demonstrated. I've written a sample program, shown in Figure 4-13, that uses SOAP to call the *GetTime* method of the Web Service. It uses the Microsoft Internet transfer control to do the actual HTTP communication. The code is somewhat unwieldy, so I haven't listed it in this book, but you will find it in the sample code on the book's Web site. Notice that, unlike the previous two examples, where the URL pointed at the method within the service, the URL used in this case is directed to the .ASMX page containing all the methods of the Web Service. The SOAP packet sent to the server contains the name of the function and its parameters, encoded in XML according to an agreed-upon schema, as you can see in the top text box. When the SOAP packet reaches the server, ASP.NET recognizes it, parses the method name and its parameters out of the packet, creates the object, and makes the call. It takes the return value of this method, formats it into XML, and returns the XML to the client.

Figure 4-13 *Sample application showing SOAP access to the Web Service*

The Web Service will accept a call via SOAP.

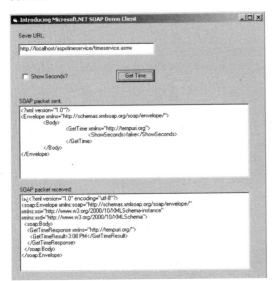

Case 4: Intelligent SOAP Proxy, Synchronous Operation

The .NET SDK provides SOAP proxy classes that make client applications much easier to write.

The SOAP example from the previous section is quite tedious to write. It reminds me somewhat of manually writing an *IDispatch* client in classic COM in the sense that there's an awful lot of boilerplate packaging that's critical to get correct (one character off and you're hosed) but which varies little from one method to the next. As Visual C++ provided wrapper classes that took the pain out of accessing Automation objects (many Visual Basic programmers never even knew it *was* painful for the C++ geeks, and the rest either didn't care or actively approved), the .NET SDK provides wrapper classes that make writing a SOAP client for your Web Service a trivial operation.

The tool that generates the proxy class is a command-line utility called Wsdl.exe, which comes with the .NET SDK. Visual Studio.NET also runs this utility from inside its development environment when you add a reference to the service. The utility reads the description of the Web Service from a WSDL file and generates a proxy for accessing its methods from the language you specify. It currently supports Visual Basic, C#, and JavaScript, but not C++. You can ask for proxies that use any of the supported protocols, but the default is SOAP. I ran Wsdl.exe with the following command line:

wsdl /l:vb http://localhost/aspxtimeservice/
timeservice.asmx?WSDL

The Visual Basic proxy class contains both synchronous and asynchronous versions of functions for getting the time from the Web Service. Figure 4-14 shows the synchronous version, which I'll discuss here. (I'll discuss the asynchronous version in the next section.)

Figure 4-14 *Visual Basic SOAP proxy class generated by WSDL.exe*

```
Public Class <System.Web.Services.WebServiceBindingAttribute
    (Name:="TimeServiceSoap", [Namespace]:="http://tempuri.org/")> TimeService
    Inherits System.Web.Services.Protocols.SoapHttpClientProtocol

    Public Sub New()
        MyBase.New
```

```
        Me.Url = "http://localhost/aspxtimeservice/timeservice.asmx"
    End Sub

    Public Function <System.Web.Services.Protocols.SoapMethodAttribute(
    "http://tempuri.org/GetTime", MessageStyle:=
    System.Web.Services.Protocols.SoapMessageStyle.ParametersInDocument)>
    GetTime(ByVal ShowSeconds As Boolean) As String
        Dim results() As Object = _
            Me.Invoke("GetTime", New Object() {ShowSeconds})
        Return CType(results(0), String)
    End Function

End Class
```

The proxy class inherits from the base class *System.Web.Services. Protocols.SoapHttpClientProtocol* (we're going to have these long, long names with us, so get used to them; at least they're descriptive), which contains the actual code. The proxy class contains a property called *Url*, which the proxy inherits from the base class. This property specifies the URL of the server to which the call is directed. It contains a default value, which it gets from the original WSDL file, but the sample program demonstrates how you can change it at run time if you want. The client calls the named method on the proxy by calling the method *Invoke*, which, again, it has inherited from the base class. This method then creates a SOAP packet containing the method name and parameters, as shown previously in Figure 4-13, and sends it to the server over HTTP. When the SOAP response packet comes back from the server, the base class parses out the return value and returns it to the proxy, which then returns it to the client.

The proxy class generated by the Wsdl.exe utility program provides prefabricated functionality for a SOAP request.

Note that the attributes block in the function name (the characters between the angle brackets) contains information that tells the base class how to package the call, such as the names of methods. Visual Studio.NET makes extensive use of these metadata attributes as a way of passing information to the prefabricated functionality of system code. In earlier days, this would probably have been done through member variables of the base class, where it would have been difficult to differentiate immutable run-time attributes from those that can change during program execution. The new arrangement is harder to mess up, which is generally a good idea.

The actual Visual Basic code for the client is shown in Figure 4-15, and the sample client application in Figure 4-16. You can see that it's trivial. The heavy lifting has been done for you by the proxy class.

Figure 4-15   *Visual Basic code used to access the synchronous method of the SOAP proxy*

```
' User clicked GetTime button.

Protected Sub button1_Click(ByVal sender As System.Object, _
                            ByVal e As System.EventArgs) _
                            Handles button1.Click

    ' Create new object of proxy class.

    Dim foo As New TimeService()

    ' Set the URL property to that specified by the user.

    foo.Url = textBox1().Text

    ' Actually call the function. Put returned result into text box
    ' for user to see.

    label1().Text = foo.GetTime(checkBox1().Checked)

End Sub
```

Figure 4-16   *Sample application that uses the SOAP proxy.*

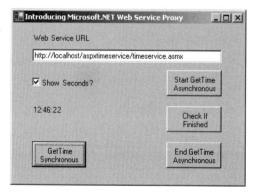

Case 5: Intelligent SOAP Proxy, Asynchronous Operation

The Internet can be a lot of fun, but it's almost always so crowded that you have no hope of enjoying it without a clever strategy for managing its chronic overload – sort of like Disney World. Even the simplest call to a Web Service can easily take 5 or 10 seconds to complete, even on a good day with the wind at your back, and the time can go up to anything from there. You can't leave a user with a frozen interface for more than a second or two, if that. An industrial-strength app can't just call the synchronous proxy method from the form button's response function, as I did in the sample. You have to somehow make the call from another thread that can wait for the response without hanging the user interface and at some later time retrieve the results from that thread and present them to the user.

Calls from a client to a Web Service usually want to run asynchronously.

Until now, most programmers have had to write their own infrastructure code to handle this situation. This type of code is notoriously tricky to get right in all cases, and the time that it took represented a dead loss in monetary terms. Now, however, since this situation is nearly universal, the intelligent proxy classes generated by Wsdl.exe are equipped with prefabricated code to handle it. Instead of making a call and blocking until it completes, your program can call one method that transmits the request data to the server and then returns immediately. At some convenient later time, your program can call another method to harvest the results returned from the server. This makes your life much, much easier because you don't have to write the scheduling code. And it works with any server, not just with those that are written to support asynchronous access.

The proxy wrapper class provides an asynchronous version of each Web Service method.

Figure 4-17 shows the asynchronous versions of the time service call. The proxy contains a method with the name *Begin[method name]*, in this case, *BeginGetTime*. Its parameter list begins with the parameters of the synchronous method—in this case, the *ShowSeconds* boolean variable. It has two more parameters used in a callback case that is deeper than I want to go in this book. Figure 4-18 shows the client code that accesses the asynchronous

You call one method that starts the request and returns immediately.

version, in which I pass *Nothing* (the Visual Basic equivalent of *null*) for both of them. The call to *BeginGetTime* starts the communication chain, sending out the request, and then returns immediately. The return value is an object of type *IAsyncResult*, which we will use in fetching the result later. We can now go off and do whatever else we want. When testing this in the lab, I inserted a long iterative loop in my .ASMX page, just counting from one to a billion to simulate a long operation. You'll have to do that yourself if you want to test this.

Figure 4-17 *The asynchronous methods of the SOAP proxy*

```
Public Function BeginGetTime(ByVal ShowSeconds As Boolean, _
                            ByVal callback As System.AsyncCallback, _
                            ByVal asyncState As Object) _
                            As System.IAsyncResult
    Return Me.BeginInvoke("GetTime", New Object() {ShowSeconds}, _
                            callback, asyncState)
End Function

Public Function EndGetTime(ByVal asyncResult As System.IAsyncResult) _
                            As String
    Dim results() As Object = Me.EndInvoke(asyncResult)
    Return CType(results(0), String)
End Function
```

Figure 4-18 *Visual Basic code used to access the asynchronous methods of the SOAP proxy*

```
' Commence the asynchronous call to get the time.

Dim AsyncTimeServiceProxy As TimeService
Dim AsyncResult As IAsyncResult

Private Sub button2_Click(ByVal sender As System.Object, _
                        ByVal e As System.EventArgs) _
                        Handles button2.Click
    AsyncTimeServiceProxy = New TimeService()
    AsyncTimeServiceProxy.Url = textBox1().Text
    AsyncResult = _
        AsyncTimeServiceProxy.BeginGetTime(checkBox1().Checked, _
                                            Nothing, Nothing)
End Sub
```

```
' Check to see whether the operation has completed.

Private Sub button3_Click(ByVal sender As System.Object, _
                          ByVal e As System.EventArgs) _
                          Handles button3.Click
    If (AsyncResult.IsCompleted = True) Then
        MessageBox.Show("Is complete")
    Else
        MessageBox.Show("NOT complete")
    End If
End Sub


' Harvest the results of the asynchronous call for getting the time.

Private Sub button4_Click(ByVal sender As System.Object, _
                          ByVal e As System.EventArgs) _
                          Handles button4.Click
    label1().Text = AsyncTimeServiceProxy.EndGetTime(AsyncResult)
    AsyncResult = Nothing
    AsyncTimeServiceProxy = Nothing
End Sub
```

At some later point, we want to harvest the results of the operation and find out what the time actually was when the server sent it back to us. We do that by calling the *End[method name]* method on the proxy, in this case *EndGetTime*, passing the *IAsyncResult* that we got from the *Begin* method. That's how the infrastructure code knows which result to give back to us, as the client can have several outstanding requests at the same time. The *End* method harvests the result and returns it.

You call another method that harvests the result when the operation is complete.

But how do we know when the operation is complete and the results ready for us to harvest? The *IAsyncResult* object contains a method used for just this purpose, named *IsCompleted*, which returns TRUE or FALSE. We can poll periodically to see whether it's done. If we call *EndGetTime* before the operation is finished, it will block until the operation does in fact complete. While you

You can check when the operation is complete by polling a property.

probably don't want to do this from your main user interface thread, it might make sense to call it from a worker thread that has reached a point in its processing past which it can't proceed without the results of the Web Service call.

Web Service Support in Visual Studio.NET

The Web Service example I showed earlier demonstrated that writing Web Services does not depend on fancy programming environments. But since developer time is the second-greatest constraint in software development (boneheaded managers who don't know which end of a soldering iron to hold being number one), it makes sense to write our Web Services using tools that will help us crank them out faster. Since our old friend Notepad lacks such useful features as an integrated debugger, Visual Studio.NET is usually a better choice for writing Web Services. I'll show you how to write a similar service using an early Beta 2 candidate release of Visual Studio.NET.

When you select File/New/Project from the Visual Studio main menu, it offers you the dialog box shown in Figure 4-19. I selected Visual Basic Projects in the left pane and the Web Service icon in the right pane, entered a project name in the edit control, and clicked OK. Visual Studio.NET generated a new solution containing the files shown in Figure 4-20. (By the way, I hate the term "solution." I consider it a MINFU. It doesn't describe what the thing does, someone probably just thought it "would be nice." It first appeared in Visual J++ 6 and seems to have metastasized into early builds of Visual Studio.NET. Since it—I won't use the 's' word again—seems to hold one or more projects, Project Group would be a far more descriptive term.)

The interesting programming takes place in the code behind file Service1.asmx, in which the code that implements your Web Service actually lives. The code for my sample Web Service is shown in Figure 4-21. Features such as auto-complete made it much easier to write with Visual Studio.NET than it was with Notepad.

Figure 4-19 *Creating a Web Service project using the New Project dialog box*

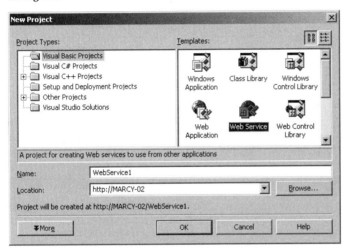

Figure 4-20 *The Solution Explorer window showing the Time Web Service files*

Visual Studio.NET can generate the files needed for a Web Service.

Figure 4-21 *Web Service code in Service1.asmx*

```
Imports System.Web.Services


Public Class Service1
    Inherits System.Web.Services.WebService

#Region " Web Services Designer Generated Code "

    'Required by the WebServices Designer.
    Private components As System.ComponentModel.Container

    Public Sub New()
        MyBase.New()

        'CODEGEN: This procedure is required by the WebServices Designer.
        'Do not modify it using the code editor.
        InitializeComponent()

        'Add your own initialization code after the InitializeComponent
        'call.
    End Sub

    Private Sub InitializeComponent()
        'CODEGEN: This procedure is required by the WebServices Designer.
        'Do not modify it using the code editor.
        components = New System.ComponentModel.Container()
    End Sub

    Overrides Sub Dispose()
        'CODEGEN: This procedure is required by the WebServices Designer.
        'Do not modify it using the code editor.
    End Sub

#End Region

    <WebMethod()> Public Function GetTime(ByVal ShowSeconds As Boolean) _
                                    As String
        If (ShowSeconds = True) Then
            Return Now().ToLongTimeString
        Else
            Return Now().ToShortTimeString
        End If
    End Function

End Class
```

The Web Service project template generates several other files, as you saw in Figure 4-20. The file Web.config is an XML data file that contains various configuration options that tell ASP.NET how to handle your Web Service at run time. We saw this file previously in Chapter 3. For example, it contains the ASP.NET session timeout interval. Currently you have to edit this file manually, but it obviously cries for a smooth configuration tool, perhaps based on Microsoft Management Console (MMC). I'd look for one to be developed before the final release of this software.

The file WebService1.vsdisco is an XML data file that is used for controlling dynamic discovery of the Web Service by clients. The default configuration, which you can see in the downloaded code, simply contains entries that tell ASP.NET to exclude certain subdirectories (generated in the publishing process) from the WSDL file that it generates. This file is not well documented at this stage of project development.

The .ASMX file is the target for client requests. Unlike the previous example, in which the code lived in this file, this example contains a callout to code that lives elsewhere, as shown in the following code. The *Codebehind* attribute tells the client where to find the code that backs up the service.

```
<%@ WebService Language="vb" Codebehind="Service1.asmx.vb"
    Class="WebService1.Service1" %>
```

The file Global.asax is where event handler functions live that handle project-wide events, such as Application_Start and Application_End. You put your own code in these functions, and ASP.NET will call it when the specified event takes place. The file Global.asax is the connection between these files and ASP.NET.

When you build your project, Visual Studio.NET automatically publishes it to the Web server you specify (in this case, the system default). To test the Web Service, simply start the debugger from the Visual Studio main menu. It pops up a testing page similar to the one we saw previously in Figure 4-5, which is a very smooth way to handle things. You can set breakpoints in your Web Service and debug anything. It's smooth, quick—dare I say it—fun, application development.

Web Service State Management

Web services are state-less by default.

Web Service objects in their natural state (groan) are stateless. That means that ASP.NET constructs a new instance of that object for each incoming call and destroys it at the end of the call. The result of one call is not available to the next call unless you go out of your way to make it so. This situation is somewhat analogous to just-in-time activation in COM+.

Web services can store state in ASP.NET's session-level and application-level state containers.

Sometimes this is what you want; sometimes it isn't. For my time service shown in this chapter, it probably is. Whether a client wants to show the seconds digit has no bearing on what the next client wants or should get. Each function call is sufficient unto itself; there's no reason to remember anything from one to the next. In the classic sense of an object as a combination of data and the code that operates on the data, you might argue that there's no object here. The client is simply making a call that has no relation to anything else, and that's not an object, that's a function. You can spend your time arguing semantics; I've got a product to ship. When this behavior isn't what you want, an object can maintain state between one call and another. The physical instance of an object is still created and destroyed on demand, but it can use ASP.NET to hold data that it was working on in its previous life, as you might leave instructions in your will for your descendants.

In Chapter 3, about ASP.NET, I discussed the two different types of state available to objects used by ASP.NET pages and the advantages and costs of both. The same state management options are available to Web Services objects. The base class *WebService*, from which your Web Service is derived, contains two collections for holding state, one called *Application* and one called *Session*. You can put data into them and take data out by accessing the collections through string names of items.

Chapter Five

Windows Forms

Below there! Oiler! What's your wark? Ye find her runnin' hard?
Ye needn't swill the cap wi' oil—this isn't the Cunard.
Ye thought? Ye are not paid to think. Go, sweat that off again!
Tck! Tck! It's deeficult to sweer nor tak' The Name in vain!

> —Rudyard Kipling, writing on the difficulty of training system
> administrators and the consequent need to supply them
> with foolproof tools. "McAndrew's Hymn," 1894.

Problem Background

This book has until now primarily discussed using Microsoft
.NET for writing server-side code, and .NET is very good for that.
However, what operating system is running on all the desktop
PCs at your business, the good one in your home that you use for
take-home work, and the old one you let the kids hack with (or
the other way around)? The laptop of the guy next to you on the
airplane? Except for a few religious Macintosh adherents and
some geeky Linux hobbyists, it's Microsoft Windows. It seems
to me that developers often forget that Windows runs on many
more client machines than it ever will on servers, probably by a
factor of 100 or more. Did those users choose Windows for its
transaction throughput or scalability to server farms? No. They
chose it because it has a good user interface and lots of available
desktop software. It's the largest software market in the world
and will be for the foreseeable future. We'll be writing different
types of desktop applications from what we wrote a decade ago.
Spreadsheets and word processors have been pretty much
beaten into the ground, but we'll still be writing for the

The Windows desktop
software market is the
largest in the world and
will remain so for the
foreseeable future.

Windows desktop. For example, we'll be writing more rich front ends for Internet applications, such as the Napster music search program that I showed you in Chapter 4.

Some of the architectural problems that desktop developers face are different from those of server developers. For example, a desktop developer deals with a single human being who reacts slowly compared to a computer, so the developer generally has plenty of CPU cycles available and doesn't have to worry about scalability the way a server developer does. On the other hand, many of the problems that desktop developers face are the same. For example, both types of developers care about reusing code that other developers wrote. They might reuse different types of code—say, code for database access vs. graphical animation—but they both face the economic necessity of leveraging the efforts of other developers. They both care about versioning. They both care about abstracting away differences between different language implementations. They both care about interoperating with COM. Desktop developers have largely ignored security until now, considering it only a server-side problem, but now that a lot of code is delivered over the Web, desktop developers now face the twin problems of authentication and authorization that have long deviled their server-side colleagues. Welcome to the real world. Developers writing desktop apps need prefabricated solutions to these problems just as server developers do.

In addition to the problems they share with server developers, desktop developers have their own set of problems. I remember writing Windows desktop apps in C about a decade ago. I spent most of my time writing code for user interface features that were common to all Windows applications. Prefabricated status bars and toolbars didn't exist then, so I had to write code for my own and so did every other developer who wanted to implement these features in an application. I had to write my own command handlers for receiving messages from controls. I still have nightmares about the time I foolishly promised a client that I'd add a print preview feature to his program for a fixed fee. It makes no sense,

Chapter Five

either economically (all that duplicated, triplicated, octuplicated programmer effort) or ergonomically (every toolbar works differently, which drives users barking mad), for every programmer to write her own implementation of all these common user interface items. We need prefabricated solutions for these common UI design problems.

Seizing the opportunity to provide standards that developers could reuse, different development environments provided different approaches to prefabricated user interfaces. Visual Basic offered a programming model based on events and forms that became quite popular for its ease of use. Visual C++ offered the Microsoft Foundation Classes (MFC), which used C++ inheritance to provide prefabricated functionality, such as the print preview feature I banged my head against so long ago. The code-based design in Visual C++ was harder to use than Visual Basic's forms-based model, but its underlying language was much more powerful. Programmers had to choose between a powerful language and rapid GUI design features. I'd often choose Visual Basic to write a front end because I liked its form editor and the ease of connecting with controls, but the wimpy language, with its arcane syntax for COM objects, its idiotic error handling, and the difficulty of calling API functions to do common tasks such as manipulate the registry would send me through the ceiling. Or I'd choose Visual C++ for its powerful language, in which case its lower-level of abstraction—for example, the difficulty of handling and firing connection point events—would send me through the ceiling.

Like everybody else in the world, desktop developers want everything, all at once, and we don't want to trade anything else away to get it. We want prefabricated solutions to the problems we share with server developers. We want rapid GUI development, but we want it to work with a powerful programming language, ideally the powerful programming language of our choice. And, for consistency's sake, we want it all to use the same programming model. And we want it to cost relatively little. As long as we're writing to Santa Claus, it couldn't hurt to at least *ask* for a pony.

Most GUI applications require a common set of features, opening the way for prefabricated functionality.

A programmer often chose a particular programming language because of its prefabricated user interface support rather than its fit to the problem domain.

As usual, we want everything but our business logic done for us (and I wouldn't mind if someone did that, too).

Solution Architecture

Many .NET CLR features help both server and desktop developers.

As you've seen in this book, .NET provides good prefabricated functionality for solving the problems common to desktop developers as well as those that server developers deal with. I covered the problems that are common to both in Chapter 2. Desktop developers will use and like the Common Language Runtime (CLR) code-reuse model, its versioning and memory management capabilities, its easy deployment of private assemblies, its organization of the system namespace, its security features, and its interoperation with COM. Web Services, described in Chapter 4, will give desktop developers something to design products for and a way of connecting to the server back end.

Windows Forms is a package that provides prefabricated user interface elements as part of the CLR.

Microsoft .NET also provides a rich set of functionality to desktop developers, which goes by the stunningly uninformative name of *Windows Forms*. Windows Forms provides .NET classes that contain prefabricated user interface components for many of the features common to most desktop apps. If you think of a cross between Visual Basic and MFC, implemented in .NET and thus

Warning

The user interface tools in Windows Forms are double-edged, as are all powerful tools. You can use them to write excellent user interfaces or terrible ones. As war is too important to be left to generals, so user interface design is too important to be left to programmers. Anyone who designs a user interface without reading the fundamental texts, *About Face* by Alan Cooper (IDG, 1995) and *The Design of Everyday Things* by Donald Norman (Doubleday, 1990), is committing malpractice. And reading *Web Pages That Suck*, by Vincent Flanders and Michael Willis (Sybex, 1998) might save you from producing some.

available to any language, you'll have about the right mental model. Windows Forms provides support for such features as menus, toolbars, and status bars; printing and print preview; hosting of ActiveX controls; and easy access to databases and Web Services. It is such a large, rich set of functionality that this chapter can only provide the barest skim of its surface. Doing justice to Windows Forms would require an entire book devoted solely to it, and I'm told that Charles Petzold is in fact writing just such a book for Microsoft Press (coming in the fall of 2001).

Simplest Example

As always, I started my exploration of Windows Forms by writing the simplest example I could think of, shown in Figure 5-1. You can download the code from this book's web site (*http://www.introducingmicrosoft.net*) and work along with me. Visual Studio.NET is a great tool for creating this type of project, and I have used it in other examples in this chapter, but to underline the tool and language independence of Windows Forms, I wrote this Visual Basic example in Notepad. The app will seem trivial, and I wrote very little code for it, but you will see that it demonstrates several of the most basic and important features of Windows Forms.

Figure 5-1 *A simple Windows Forms sample.*

A Windows Forms sample, written in Visual Basic using Notepad, begins here.

Figure 5-2 shows the code for my sample app. You'll notice that I didn't import any namespaces in this example. (See Chapter 2 for an explanation of namespaces.) I never have to do that if I don't want to; it's simply a matter of convenience when I want to call objects by their short names instead of their fully qualified names. I decided to do the latter in this case so that you can see exactly where each object comes from. You do need to include some system DLLs in the compilation by reference, which you can see in the compilation batch file in the downloaded source code. Visual Studio.NET automatically does this if you use it for a Windows Forms project.

The sample doesn't bother to import namespaces.

A top-level window in Windows Forms is called a *form,* and every application needs to have at least one. This requirement will be familiar to Visual Basic programmers. C++ programmers should think of this form as their application's main window. Windows Forms provides a prefabricated implementation of the basic functionality that every top-level window needs to have in the CLR base class *System.Windows.Forms.Form.* This base class provides such features as hosting controls, supporting the docking of child windows, and responding to events.

We derive our own form class from a CLR base class that provides basic prefabricated form functionality.

I start out this simple app by deriving a new class, called *SimplestHelloWorld,* from this base class. By using this inheritance notation, I tell the compiler to take all the functionality of the base class that Microsoft wrote and include it by reference in my new derived class. (See Chapter 2 for a further discussion of inheritance.)

We override the base class's constructor to tack on new functionality when our form is created.

Now that we have our new class representing our own top-level window, we need to write code that says how our object differs from the base class. In this case, we override the base class's *New* method (known as a constructor, you'll remember from Chapter 2), which is called whenever an instance of our object is created. In this method, we first call our base class's constructor, thereby allowing the base class to complete its initialization before we attempt anything in our derived class. Failing to do this is a common cause of bugs in object-oriented programming. This call is not made automatically by the framework because occasionally you want to omit it or point it somewhere else, for example in cases where you are completely replacing some part of the base class's functionality instead of piggy-backing on it as we are doing here. The base class contains a property named *Text*, which represents the string in the form's title bar. We set that property to a distinctive title that we will recognize.

Figure 5-2 *Simplest sample app's code listing.*

```
Namespace IMDN.SimplestHelloWorld

' Declare a new class that derives from the CLR base
' class System.Windows.Forms.Form.

Public Class SimplestHelloWorld : Inherits System.Windows.Forms.Form

    ' Class constructor. Forward call to the base class for
    ' its initialization, and then set our window's caption.

    Public Sub New()
        MyBase.New
        Me.Text = "Introducing Microsoft.Net: Hello World"
    End Sub

    ' This function is the entry point for a Windows Forms
    ' application. Create a new instance of our form
    ' object, and then pass that to the system function that
    ' runs the application.

    Shared Sub Main()
        System.Windows.Forms.Application.Run(New SimplestHelloWorld())
    End Sub

End Class

End Namespace
```

We create an instance of our form object and tell the loader to run it.

We now need to hook up our top-level form so that the system loader will know which form to show when the program starts running. Visual Studio.NET would add this code to the project for us automatically if we were using it. Since we're not, it's up to us to add the code. When a program starts up, the loader looks for a function called *Main*, which you will see I've placed in our object. Only your startup form can contain this method, and the loader will call it only once. The qualifier *Shared* means that there is only one instance of this function shared among all objects of the class (*static* for you C++ geeks). The CLR loader calls this function to start the application. It is up to you to put in this function whatever code you need to make the application go. A Windows Forms application requires a thread to run a message loop that receives user interface messages (such as keystrokes and mouse clicks) from the operating system and routes them to the correct event handlers. The static CLR function *System.Windows.Forms. Application.Run* creates and starts exactly such a thread. We pass this function a new instance of our form object to tell it which form to send the messages to.

More Complex Example: Controls and Events

Our simplest application demonstrated a few necessary features, but other than that it's extremely boring. Our form doesn't even have an OK button. I will now demonstrate a less trivial example, a screen shot of which is shown in Figure 5-3. I've switched to Visual Studio.NET for this example, even though I didn't have to, because its editor makes manipulating the controls much easier.

Figure 5-3 *A more complex form created with Visual Studio.NET.*

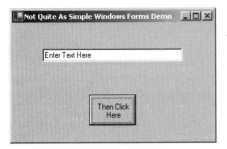

A more complex Windows Forms example starts here.

You will find that the Windows Forms programming model closely resembles the Visual Basic 6.0 programming model, although it's available to any CLR language. That's a good idea because Visual Basic's programming model was and is immensely popular. It's the language behind it that many programmers can't stand, myself included, and now we can use any CLR-compliant language that we want. Besides, the C++ guys won most of the arm wrestling over the object programming model discussed in Chapter 2. An optimist would say that Microsoft was blending the best features of two design philosophies. A pessimist would say that Visual Basic programmers needed a consolation prize.

Forms usually contain controls to obtain input from and display output to the user. The CLR Windows Forms package contains a rich set of controls, just as Visual Basic 6.0 does. In writing this sample program, I dragged controls from the Visual Studio.NET toolbox onto my form, as shown in Figure 5-4. When I did this, Visual Studio.NET generated code in my form that makes CLR calls that create the controls, set their properties, and place them at the proper position when the form is first created. An excerpted version of this method is shown in Figure 5-5.

Figure 5-4 *The Visual Studio.NET toolbox.*

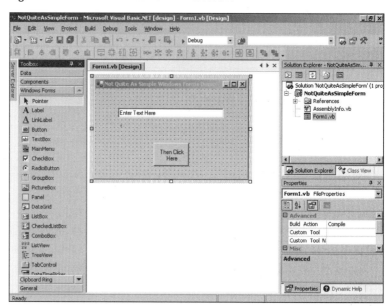

Figure 5-5 *Excerpted version of the* InitializeComponent *method showing control creation.*

```
Private WithEvents Button1 As System.Windows.Forms.Button
Private WithEvents TextBox1 As System.Windows.Forms.TextBox

'NOTE: The following procedure is required by the Windows Forms Designer.
'It can be modified using the Windows Forms Designer.
'Do not modify it using the code editor.

Private Sub InitializeComponent()

    ' Create controls.

    Me.Button1 = New System.Windows.Forms.Button()
    Me.TextBox1 = New System.Windows.Forms.TextBox()

    ' Set button properties.

    Me.Button1.Location = New System.Drawing.Point(112, 96)
    Me.Button1.Size = New System.Drawing.Size(75, 40)
    Me.Button1.TabIndex = 1
    Me.Button1.Text = "Then Click Here"
```

```
' Set text box properties.

Me.TextBox1.Location = New System.Drawing.Point(48, 48)
Me.TextBox1.Text = "Enter Text Here"
Me.TextBox1.TabIndex = 0
Me.TextBox1.Size = New System.Drawing.Size(200, 20)

' Set form properties.

Me.Text = "Not Quite As Simple Windows Forms Demo"
Me.Controls.AddRange(New System.Windows.Forms.Control() _
    {Me.TextBox1, Me.Button1})

End Sub
```

For the editor's logistical convenience, this code lives in a private method called *InitializeComponent*, which is called from the form's constructor. In Visual Basic.NET, the controls on a form are created by code that you can actually see, instead of by some invisible hand behind the scenes, as they were in Visual Basic 6.0. The new controls are also added to a collection called *Controls*, which our form inherited from its base class. This collection allows a form to keep track of all of its controls.

Controls on a form are created by CLR function calls.

The controls fire events to their containers in response to their interaction with the human user. For example, a button control fires an event signaling a click. We need to write event handler functions that will get called when the control signals an event. We do this by adding a method called *<Control_name>_<Event_name>* to the form class, in this case, *Button1_Click*, shown in Figure 5-6. Visual Studio.NET does this for us when we click on the button control in the editor, but anyone writing code in Notepad could simply add the method to the form class's code. When the control fires an event, the CLR's event mechanism looks for a handler function sporting the proper name for that event from that control and calls it if it finds one. You can also add an event handler dynamically as your code executes via the Visual Basic function *AddHandler*, not described here.

Controls fire events to handlers in your code.

Figure 5-6 *Event handler for a button click.*

```
' User clicked the button. Display a message box containing the
' text currently in the text box.

Private Sub Button1_Click(ByVal sender As Object, _
                            ByVal e As System.EventArgs)
    MessageBox.Show("You entered: " + textBox1().Text)
End Sub
```

A form supports the *Dispose* method for deterministic finalization.

Forms support deterministic finalization, which I discussed in the section about garbage collection in Chapter 2. The base class *System.Windows.Forms.Form* contains a method called *Dispose* that allows a client to immediately liquidate a form and free its resources without having to wait for or cause a complete garbage collection. This is especially important in Windows Forms because every form contains an operating system window handle for each control it contains, plus one for the form itself. These window handles are somewhat scarce in Windows 95 and Windows 98 (don't get me started), and deterministic finalization allows a client to release these resources as soon as it is finished with a form. You will see when you examine the source code that Visual Studio.NET automatically overrides this method, adding code that calls the *Dispose* method of all the controls that the form contains.

Writing Your Own Windows Forms Control

As you can see, developing good Windows Forms applications requires having good controls. While the CLR provides many good and useful controls, this set represents only a tiny fraction of the possible things that users might want to do. We'd really like to be able to write our own Windows controls, either for sale or for internal use. And we'd like a marketplace to develop so that third-party vendors can write their own controls and we can buy them. For this to happen, we need good prefabricated support in the CLR for writing new controls.

We need to be able to write our own .NET controls.

The notion of distributing reusable software containing user interface elements, methods, properties, and events in a convenient package that plugs into a smart environment for rapid development has been fantastically successful in the software marketplace. It started with 16-bit VBX controls and moved to ActiveX controls when Windows moved to 32 bits. The pages of *MSDN Magazine* and the *Visual Basic Programmer's Journal* are crammed with ads for ActiveX controls providing everything from spreadsheets and spelling checkers to strip chart recorders and electrocardiograms. They've multiplied like rabbits competing with marsupials in Australia. If .NET is to be successful, it must allow this marketplace to continue to prosper.

> The third-party market for prefabricated controls has been fantastically successful.

Windows Forms provides support for developing your own Windows Forms controls. The level of support is far too large a topic for this book to cover in any depth, but I did write a quick sample to demonstrate the ease with which you can write your own controls. A Windows Forms client hosting the control is shown in Figure 5-7, and the control's code is listed in Figure 5-8. Someone could probably milk this topic for a whole book, if he bulked it up with lots of code listings and screen shots (oops).

Figure 5-7 *Windows Forms control in Windows Forms client.*

Figure 5-8 *Excerpted code listing of Windows Forms control.*

```
Public Class UserControl1

    ' Our control inherits from the CLR base class UserControl.

    Inherits System.Windows.Forms.UserControl


    ' Our control exposes a public property called "ShowSeconds".

    Private myShowSeconds As Boolean

    Public Property ShowSeconds() As Boolean
        Get
            Return myShowSeconds
        End Get

        Set
            myShowSeconds = Value
        End Set
    End Property

    ' We override the OnPaint handler to do our own painting.

    Protected Overrides Sub OnPaint(ByVal e As _
                                    System.Windows.Forms.PaintEventArgs)
        < code omitted>
    End Sub

End Class
```

A Windows Forms control example begins here.

You write a Windows Forms control by deriving a class from the base class *System.Windows.Forms.UserControl.* Creating a Windows Control Library project in Visual Studio.NET does this for you. C++ developers who wrote ActiveX controls by deriving from the MFC base class *COleControl* will find this approach familiar. This base class contains the functionality that is common to all Windows Forms controls, from simple properties such as a background color to sophisticated negotiations with its container, such as those required for floating and docking. Your control overrides the Windows Forms event handlers whose behavior you want

Writing a Windows Forms control is dead easy inheriting from a prefabricated CLR base class.

to replace, in this case the *OnPaint* notification, in which I write CLR calls that paint my control's rectangle in my control's background color and draw the current time on it using my control's default font. That's really all there was to writing this control. You put the control in your Visual Studio toolbox by right-clicking on the toolbox, picking Customize Toolbox from the shortcut menu, and then selecting the control, as shown in Figure 5-9.

Figure 5-9 *Adding a Windows Forms control to the Visual Studio.NET toolbox.*

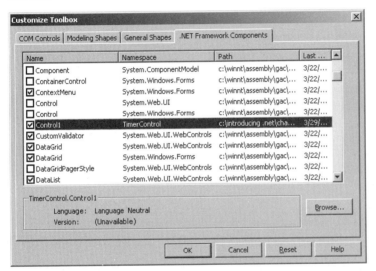

But if I write a Windows Forms control, doesn't that mean only .NET applications can use it? There aren't many of them out there, at least not yet, so shouldn't I wait for a critical mass before I invest my development dollars? To help you answer "No" to these questions, the *UserControl* base class contains all the functionality that it needs to be accessible to ActiveX control hosts such as Visual Basic 6.0. This will allow a developer of a .NET control to take advantage of the enormous installed base and make a lot of money.

A .NET control can be used by ActiveX control hosts such as Visual Basic 6.0.

You have to write one relatively small piece of code to make your .NET control accessible to ActiveX hosts. ActiveX controls make several registry entries that standard COM servers don't, so you have to add this functionality to your .NET control. The CLR contains prefabricated functions that will make and remove these entries. These go by the names *Control.ActiveXRegister* and *Control.ActiveXUnregister*. You need to provide two functions in your control class marked with attributes that tell the .NET COM registration utility to call them during the registration process. These functions need to delegate to *ActiveXRegister* and *ActiveXUnregister*, as shown in Figure 5-10. That's the only extra piece of code that you have to write today, and I wouldn't be surprised if it moved into the base class in some future version.

You have to write one small extra piece of code to make your .NET control appear as an ActiveX control.

Figure 5-10 *Registration helper functions in a Windows Forms control. Required only if you want your control to appear as an ActiveX control to existing ActiveX hosts.*

```
Public Shared Sub <System.Runtime.InteropServices.ComRegisterFunction()>
    AxRegister(ByVal regKey As String)

    Dim foo As New UserControl1()
    ActiveXRegister(foo.GetType)
End Sub

Public Shared Sub <System.Runtime.InteropServices.ComUnregisterFunction()>
    AxUnregister(ByVal regkey As String)

    Dim foo As New UserControl1()
    ActiveXUnregister(foo.GetType)
End Sub
```

Once you've done this, using your .NET control as an ActiveX control is simply a matter of registering it as you would any other .NET class wanting to be a COM server, as discussed in Chapter 2. You must build it with the *ComVisible* attribute set to True so that it knows that COM clients are allowed to see it. The CLR must be installed on the client machine. You generate a type library and register it with the RegAsm.exe utility. You then have to put your control DLL somewhere the client application, in this case Visual Basic, can see it, either the GAC or the VB98 directory where its other binary files live. Visual Basic's control selection dialog box will then offer your .NET control as an option, as shown in Figure 5-11. You can install it and run it, as in the sample that comes with the code you can download for this chapter.

Figure 5-11 *Visual Basic 6.0 offering our Windows Forms control.*

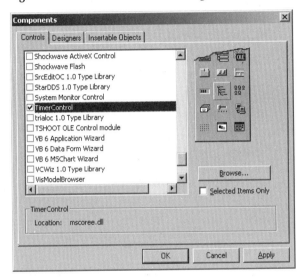

Hosting ActiveX Controls in Windows Forms

I've written previously of the enormous popularity of ActiveX controls. If .NET couldn't use them, many developers wouldn't use it, which would mean that ActiveX developers wouldn't have a large enough market to merit converting their controls, and the whole concept would be stillborn. Therefore, the developers of Windows Forms wisely decided to include support for hosting ActiveX controls. Since ActiveX controls work by means of COM, I'd strongly suggest that anyone interested in pursuing this topic go back to Chapter 2 and read the section about interoperation between COM and .NET.

Windows Forms can host ActiveX controls.

A Windows Forms application hosts an ActiveX control by generating a wrapper class similar to the runtime callable wrapper that wraps a COM object.

A Windows Forms application does not inherently know how to use an ActiveX control. It only understands controls written with its own native Windows Forms architecture. For a Windows Forms application to host an ActiveX control, you need to generate a wrapper class that will contain the ActiveX control, mediate between its COM-based world view and the .NET world view of its container, and present it to Windows Forms as if it were a native Windows Forms control. You essentially need a monster runtime callable wrapper, as described in Chapter 2, that consumes all the COM interfaces that an ActiveX control provides, while it provides the COM interfaces that an ActiveX control requires from its host. This architecture is shown in Figure 5-12. If you think that sounds like a hell of a lot of work, you're right, but don't worry because the CLR provides a prefabricated class that does it all for you, called *System.Windows.Forms.AxHost*.

Figure 5-12 *Windows Forms architecture for hosting ActiveX controls.*

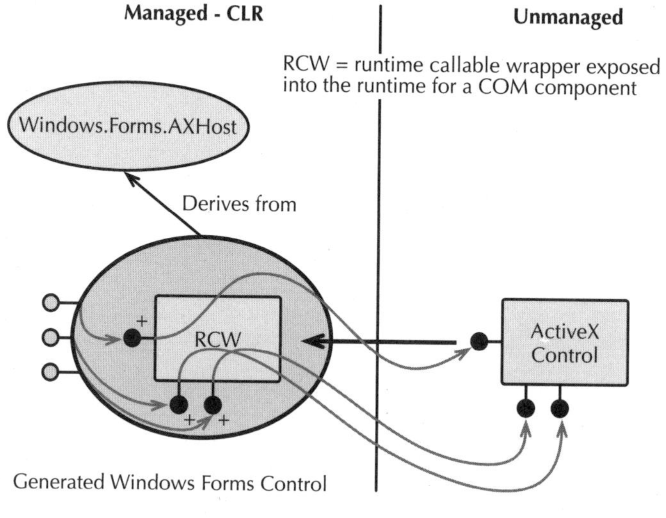

You need to derive a separate wrapper class from *AxHost* for each class of ActiveX control that your application wants to host. This class will contain the class ID or program ID used to create the

ActiveX control and will expose in a native .NET format the properties, methods, and events of the internal ActiveX control. This will feel familiar to anyone who has ever imported an ActiveX control into Visual C++ or Visual J++. You generate this wrapper class using a command-line utility call AxImp.exe that comes with the .NET SDK. If you are using Visual Studio.NET, you can simply right-click on the toolbox, pick Customize Toolbox from the shortcut menu, and you will see the dialog box in Figure 5-13, which offers the list that Microsoft calls *COM Controls*. (So long "ActiveX," and good riddance. One less MINFU in the world.)

You create the wrapper class using Visual Studio.NET or a command-line utility.

Figure 5-13 *Dialog box offering choice of ActiveX controls to import into your project.*

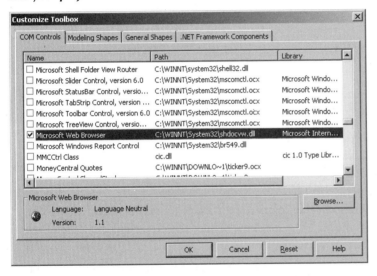

When you select a control from this list, Visual Studio.NET runs AxImp.exe internally and generates this wrapper class for you. It's built into a separate DLL as part of your project. You can't see the source code directly, at least not currently, but you can view its methods and properties in the Object Browser, shown in Figure 5-14. The new control will appear on your toolbox, and you can use it in the familiar manner.

Figure 5-14   *Visual Studio.NET Object Browser showing methods and properties of generated wrapper class for Web Browser ActiveX control.*

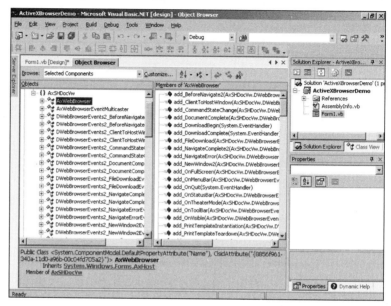

I've written a sample Windows Forms program that uses the Microsoft Web Browser ActiveX control. Figure 5-15 shows a screen shot of it, displaying this book's Web page.

I imported the ActiveX control into Visual Studio.NET as described previously. I then placed the control on my form and wrote the code shown in Figure 5-16. When the user clicks the Fetch button, I call the wrapper class's *Navigate* method, passing the URL that the user has entered. The wrapper class transforms this call into a COM call and passes it to the wrapped ActiveX control.

Figure 5-15 *Windows Forms application using Web Browser ActiveX control.*

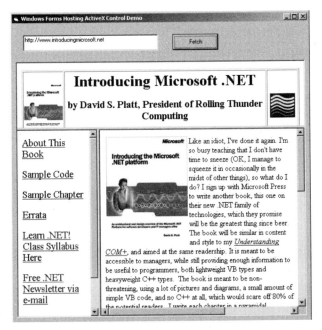

Figure 5-16 *Windows Forms ActiveX sample code.*

```
' Call method on our wrapper class control as if it
' were a native Windows Forms control.

Protected Sub Button1_Click(ByVal sender As Object, _
                    ByVal e As System.EventArgs)
    AxWebBrowser1.Navigate(TextBox1.Text, 0, "", "", "")
End Sub
```

Here is a sample application showing an ActiveX control hosted in a Windows Forms application.

```vb
    Public Sub New()
        MyBase.New()

        'CODEGEN: This procedure is required by the WebServices Designer
        'Do not modify it using the code editor.
        InitializeComponent()

        'Add your own initialization code after the InitializeComponent
        'call
    End Sub

    Private Sub InitializeComponent()
        'CODEGEN: This procedure is required by the WebServices Designer
        'Do not modify it using the code editor.
        components = New System.ComponentModel.Container()
    End Sub

    Overrides Sub Dispose()
        'CODEGEN: This
```

`#End Region`

```vb
<WebMethod()> P                           yVal ShowSes
                                                As String

If (S
```

Epilogue and Benediction

… in spite o' knock and scale, o' friction, waste an' slip,
An' by that light-now, mark my word—we'll build the Perfect Ship.
I'll never last to judge her lines or take her curve—not I.
But I ha' lived an' I ha' worked. All thanks to Thee, Most High!
An' I ha' done what I ha' done—judge Thou if ill or well—

—Rudyard Kipling, writing on the inevitability of technological
progress, "McAndrew's Hymn," 1894

Like McAndrew, I have done what I have done—written this book—and now it's up to you to judge it. Is .NET the perfect operating system? Don't be silly. Is this the perfect book about it? Don't be sillier. We won't see perfection in our lifetimes, any more than McAndrew did. But .NET will make you more money than anything else that's out there now or on the horizon, and I hope this book helps you understand how.

My daughter, born this year, belongs to the first generation to know the Internet from the cradle, not as some recent geeky add-on, as it is for you and me. Her cousins belong to the first generation to grow up with desktop PCs, her parents to the first generation with TV, her grandparents to the first with radio. Do you have any idea how this will shape her? Of course not, neither do I; nobody does. Or rather, lots of people have mutually contradictory ideas, and no one knows who is correct. But as I write these words in 2001,

I remember Arthur C. Clarke's introduction to his book *2001: A Space Odyssey:* "It is important to remember that this is a work of fiction. The truth, *as always*, will be far stranger." He's the one guy I believe.

We software developers hold much more responsibility than we ever did before. As the dean of my engineering school, a recovering metallurgist, recently wrote in our alumni journal, "Today our nation's wealth and security resides much more in bits and bytes than it does in bullets or bullion." If Freecell crashed, who cares, except the guy who lost his string of winning games? But it's different when an airline's reservation system goes down, and more different still when a hospital loses all its patients' medical histories. As Kipling wrote, speaking of McAndrew's passengers,

> *Maybe they steam from grace to wrath—to sin by folly led,—*
> *It isna mine to judge their path—their lives are on my head.*
> *Mine at the last—when all is done it all comes back to me,*
> *The fault that leaves six thousand ton a log upon the sea.*

Carry it well.

I submit to you, my fellow geeks, that we are bringing about nothing more nor less than the next step in the evolution of our species: humankind is creating its own image. Crude, limited, buggy (and what's more human than that?), but our own image nonetheless. That's why development holds a thrill that nothing we've ever experienced can match. Some people describe it as sexual, and based on the creative output, that doesn't surprise me. McAndrew felt it 100 years ago:

> *Uplift am I? When first in store the new-made beasties stood,*
> *Were Ye cast down that breathed the Word declarin' all things good?*

That's why we got into this crazy business, and that's why we stay. That's why you see very few geeks hanging up their mice and going to law school, even with their stock options under water.

Read what Kipling wrote about McAndrew 100 years ago. For "horse-power," substitute "megaflops," or whatever your performance metric is. For "first-class passengers," put in your own description of an idiot—"bone-head manager," or perhaps "VB programmer." And tell me this is not how you feel when your system goes live:

> Oh for a man to weld it then, in one trip-hammer strain,
> Till even first-class passengers could tell the meanin' plain!
> But no one cares except mysel' that serve an' understand
> My seven thousand horse-power here. Eh, Lord! They're grand, they're grand!

```
                        Public Sub New()
                            MyBase.New()

                            'CODEGEN: This procedure is required by the WebServices Designer
                            'Do not modify it using the code editor.
                            InitializeComponent()

                            'Add your own initialization code after the InitializeComponent
                            'call.
                        End Sub

                        Private Sub InitializeComponent()
                            'CODEGEN: This procedure is required by the WebServices Designer
                            'Do not modify it using the code editor.
                            components = New System.ComponentModel.Container()
                        End Sub

                        Overrides Sub Dispose()
                            'CODEGEN: This
```

```
#End Region
```

```
<WebMethod()> P                              yVal ShowSe
                                                 As String

    If (S
```

Index

Note: Page numbers in italics refer to figures or tables.

SPECIAL CHARACTERS

A

assemblies, 36–47
  code groups and, 88–89
  concept of, 36–39, *37, 38*
  deployment and, 39–43, *41, 42, 43*
  permission sets and, 88
  private, 31–32
  versioning and, 44–47, *45, 46*
Assembly Cache Viewer, 40, *41*
Assembly Generation Utility (al.exe), 37, 39
AssemblyInfo.vb file, 45, *45*
asterisk (*), 136
asynchronous intelligent SOAP proxy classes,
  169–72
attributes, assembly, 39, 72–73, 74, 167. *See
  also* metadata
authentication, 100, 124–35. *See also* security,
  ASP.NET
  forms-based or cookie, 127–31, *127, 128, 129*
  identity and, 139–44, *141, 142, 143, 144*
  Passport-based, 131–35, *133*
  types of, 124–26, *125*
  Windows-based, 126
Authenticode system, 83–84
authorization, 135–39
AutoComplete attribute, 75
automatic memory management. *See* memory
  management
AutoPostBack property, 102
AxHost class, 194–95
aximp.exe utility, 195

B

backward compatibility, 18, 65, 162
bandwidth, Internet, 2
base classes, 49, *50*
  overriding methods of, 53–54
  Web control, 113
  Web Service, 156
  Windows Forms, 182
base object, 54
Begin[method name] method, 169–70
beta software warnings, 11–12, 113, 138
binding, COM objects and, 69

browsers
  ASP.NET pages and, 104–5
  generic Internet access and, 148–49
  Internet Explorer, 157–59, *158, 159*
  Microsoft Web Browser ActiveX control, *197*
  Object Browser, *51, 196*
  Web controls and, 112, *113*
build number, 45

C

C++
  error handling, 76
  memory management, 56–57
  object-oriented features, 48
  strings, 17
  this book and, 9–10
  Visual C++ and user interfaces, 179
C#, 10
  inheritance, 50
  overriding base class methods, 53–54
  simplest .NET Framework object client,
    28–32, *31*
  transactions, 74
caspol.exe utility, 86
Catch blocks, 77–82, *78, 79*
CCWs (COM callable wrappers), 70–73, *71, 72*
certificates, digital, 19
circular object references, 63–64
Class attribute, 156
classes
  base and derived, 49, *50*, 156 (*see also* base
    classes; inheritance)
  constructors and destructors, 54–56, 71,
    182–83
  objects and, 47–48 (*see also* objects)
  proxy (*see* proxy classes)
Class_Initialize event, 55
Class_Terminate methods, 59
cleanup code, 59–64, *64*
client applications. *See also* applications; server
  applications
  ActiveX, and Windows Forms controls,
    191–93, *193*
  assemblies and version numbers, 46–47, *46*
  impersonation, 143–44, *143, 144*

controls, Windows Forms
events and, 184–88, *185, 186*
writing custom, 188–93, *189, 191, 193*
Controls collection, 187
cookie authentication, 127–31, *127, 128, 129*
role authorization and, 138–39
CopyLocal property, 42–43
costs
authentication systems, 124
Internet hardware and bandwidth, 2
.NET Framework, 23–24
performance (*see* performance)
versioning problems, 44
cross-language inheritance, 54
cryptography, public key, 38, 40–41, 43
culture, assembly, 38
custom assembly attributes, 39
custom Windows Forms controls, 188–93, *189, 191, 193*

D

databases
access services, 7, 9
security identity and, 139–44, *141, 142, 143, 144*
session state in SQL, 122
transactions, 73–75
DataGrid method, 62
data tier security identity, 139–44, *141, 142, 143, 144*
DateTime class, 28
DeactivateOnReturn property, 75
dedicated applications, 8–9, 148
default constructors, CCWs and, 71
default permission sets, *87*
default versioning behavior, 46
<deny> element, 136
deployment, 7–8
assemblies and, 39–43, *41, 42, 43*
Web Services and, 158–59
derived classes, 49, *50,* 156. *See also* inheritance
Design of Everyday Things, The (Norman), 180

desktop PCs, 1
networked PCs vs., 1
security and, 3
Windows and software market for, 177–79
destructors, class, 54–55, 59
deterministic finalization, 61–64, *64,* 80–81, 188
developers
desktop PCs and, 177–79
infrastructure and, 5–6
DHTML, 112
digital certificates, 19
digital signatures, 83–84
directories
ASP.NET configuration files and, 114–15, *115*
authorization and, 136
client application, 31
global assembly cache, 40
security policy settings, 86
Web Services and, 154
DisableCommit method, 75
display controls, 111–12
Dispose method, 62–63, 80, 188
distributed computing, 4
distribution, Web and software, 2, 82–83
DLL Hell, 44
DLLs. *See also* applications
.NET Framework object server, 25–28, 31
System namespace, 34
domains, 136, *137*
dynamic Web pages, 94–96, *94. See also* ASP.NET

E

early binding, 69
EnableCommit method, 75
encryption, 4, 38, 40–41, 43
authentication and, 125–26
End[method name] method, 171–72
enterprise level security, 86
environment, run-time, 7–8, 96
Equals method, 52, *52*
error handling, structured, 75–82, *77, 79*

event handlers
  Web control, 103–4
  Web Service, 175
  Windows Forms, 187–88
  Windows Forms controls, 190–91
events, Windows Forms, 184–88, *185, 186*
examples. *See* applications, simplest example
Exception class, 79–81
exception handling, structured, 75–82, *77, 79*
EXEs, simplest .NET Framework object client, 28–32, *31. See also* applications

F

Feynman, Richard, 131–32
file-level authorization, 136
FileNotFoundException exception, 81
files
  ASMX (*see* Web Services)
  ASPX (*see* ASP.NET)
  assemblies (*see* assemblies)
  authorization and, 136
  database (*see* databases)
  directories (*see* directories)
  configuration (*see* configuration; web.config files)
  registry (*see* registry settings)
  System namespace, 34
  utilities (*see* utilities)
  WSDL (Web Service Descriptor Language), 159–62, *162*
finalization, deterministic, 61–64, *64,* 80–81, 188
Finalize method, 60
finalizer methods, 60, 59–61, 80–81
Finally blocks, 80–81
"fire-and-forget" memory management, 57
folders. *See* directories
Form class, 182, 188
forms
  Windows Forms, 182
  Visual Basic, 102
forms-based authentication, 127–31, *127, 128, 129*
  role authorization and, 138–39

Framework. *See* .NET Framework
fully qualified names, 34–35, 182
functions. *See also* methods
  exposing server, 8–9
  global, 32, 47
  namespaces and organizing system, 19, 22, 32–36

G

GAC (global assembly cache), 40–43, *41*
  CCWs and, 71
  versions in, 46
  Windows Forms controls and, 193
gacutil.exe utility, 40
garbage collection
  automatic memory management and, 58 (*see also* memory management)
  COM objects and, 34–35, 68–69
  destructors and, 54–55
  exception handling and, 80
  .NET Framework and, 7, 22
  performance and, 24
  Windows Forms and, 188
GetObjectContext function, 75
GetTypeFromCLSID method, 69
GetTypeFromProgID method, 69
Global.asax file, 175
global assembly cache. *See* GAC (global assembly cache)
global functions, 32, 47
Grosch's law, 13, 24
groups, code, 88–89
GUI (Graphic User Interface) applications, 179. *See also* user interfaces

H

hardware, Internet, 2. *See also* desktop PCs
hashing, assembly, 43
hosting ActiveX controls in Windows Forms, 193–97, *194, 195, 196, 197*
Hotmail, 133–34

HTML
  ASP.NET and, 8, 98 (*see also* ASP.NET)
  controls, 106
  DHTML, 112
HTTP
  encryption and, 126
  Web Services and, 152–53, *153, 154*
HTTP GET requests, 161, *162,* 163, *163*
HTTP POST requests, 161, 163–64, *164*

I

IAsynResult objects, 170, 171
identity, 139–44, *141, 142, 143, 144. See also*
  authentication
<identity> element, 140, *141*
Identity property, 141
IDispatch interface, 69
IDisposable interface, 62
IIdentity interface, 141
IIS (Internet Information Services), 8, 97, 126,
  154
IL (Microsoft Intermediate Language), 20–21,
  21, 28
ILDASM.exe (IL Disassembler), 38, *38,* 45, *45,*
  46, 50
Impersonate function, 144
impersonation attribute, 143, *144*
impersonation-delegation model, 143–44,
  143, 144
importing namespaces, 26, 30, 35
  inheritance vs., 157
Imports directive, 26, 35, 67, 156, 157
informational version, 46
infrastructure
  COM, 16
  Microsoft .NET as prefabricated, 7–9
  problems, 2–5 (*see also* problems,
    architectural; solution architecture)
  software developers and, 5–6
inheritance
  importing namespaces vs., 157
  .NET Framework, 49–54, *50, 51, 52*
  Visual Basic, 156–57, 182
  Visual Basic and COM, 18–19

Inherits keyword, 50, 157
InitializeComponent method, 187
input, Web page, 95, 98–99. *See also* Web
  controls
input controls, 110–11
integrity, assembly, 43
integrity, database, 73
intelligent SOAP proxy classes
  asynchronous, 169–72
  synchronous, 166–68, *168*
interfaces, COM, 16–17, 62, 69
Internet
  infrastructure and, 3
  software (*see* software)
  user interaction model, 147
  Web and, 1–2 (*see also* Web)
Internet Explorer, 157–59, *158, 159*
Internet Information Services (IIS), 8, 97, 126,
  154
interoperability, COM. *See* COM
  interoperability
interoperability, platform, 17, 21
intranets, Windows authentication and, 126
InvokeMember function, 69
Invoke method, 167
IPrincipal interface, 138
IsCompleted method, 171
IsInRole method, 138, 141
ISupportErrorInfo and *IErrorInfo* interfaces, 76

J

Jablokow's corollary, 13
Java
  error handling, 76
  memory management, 57
  object-oriented features, 48
  strings, 17
just-in-time (JIT) compilation, 21, 30–31, 100
Just So Stories (Kipling), 12

K

Kerberos authentication system, 126
Kipling, Rudyard, 12–14, 15, 93, 147, 177

postback data, 111
Pournelle's Law (Jerry Pournelle), 11
prerelease software warnings, 11–12, 113, 138
Principles of Transaction Processing (Bernstein and Newcomer), 73
private assemblies, 31–32, 39–40
privileges, code access, 84–85
problems, architectural. *See also* solution architecture
  ASP.NET and, 93–96, *94*
  COM and, 16–17
  infrastructure and, 2–5
  .NET Framework and, 15–20
  this book and, 11
  Web Services and, 147–51, *150*
  Windows Forms, 177–79
processes
  security identity and, 139–44, *141, 142, 143, 144*
  session state and, 121–22
process management, 145–46
processModel element, 146, *146*
programming. *See also* applications; code
  code access security, 90–91
  identity authorization, 141–42, 143–44, *144*
  Internet access, 149–51 (*see also* Web Services)
  languages (*see* languages, programming)
  model, ASP.NET as, 8
  user interfaces (*see* Windows Forms)
  utilities (*see* utilities)
program zones, 89
projects. *See also* applications
  configuring Web application, 113–16, *115, 116*
  Visual Studio (*see* Microsoft Visual Studio.NET)
protocols
  SOAP (*see* SOAP (Simple Object Access Protocol))
  HTTP, 126, 152–53, *153, 154*
  Web Service, 161 (*see also* client applications, Web Services)
proxy classes
  asynchronous, 166–68, *168*
  synchronous, 169–70
  Web Services, 153, *154*
public key cryptography, 38, 40–41, 43
public methods, *System.Object, 52*

Q

qualified names, 34–35, 182
question mark (?), 137
Quicken, 3–4

R

raw SOAP protocol, 164–65, *165*
RCWs (runtime callable wrappers), 65–70, *65, 66, 67, 69*
recycling, process, 145–46
RedirectFromLoginPage function, 130
reference counting, 57, 63–64
references to shared assemblies, 42–43, *43*
regasm.exe utility, 71–72, 192
registry settings, 8
  CCWs and, 71–72, *72*
  COM configuration, 114
  private assemblies and, 39
  transactions and, 74
  for Windows Forms controls, 192
regsvcs.exe utility, 74
ReleaseComObject function, 34–35, *68*
requestLimit attribute, 146
resource recovery. *See* memory management
restarting systems, 145–46
Return keyword, 28
return values, errors as, 76
reuse, code, 7, 49. *See also* inheritance
revision number, 45
Richter, Jeffrey, 39–40, 60
robustness, 145
roles, authorization, 137–39
Run function, 184
runtime callable wrappers (RCWs), 65–70, *65, 66, 67, 69*
run-time compilation, 21, 30–31, 100
run-time environment, 7–8, 96

S

sample code, 9–10. *See also* applications, simplest example

Windows Forms, *continued*
  problem background, 177–79
  simplest example, 181–84, *181*
  solution architecture, 180–81
  user interface design and, 180
  writing custom controls, 188–93, *189, 191,*
    193
worker processes
  process recycling and, 145–46
  session state and, 121
wrapper classes, ActiveX controls and, 194,
  194
Write function, 30, 34
wsdl.exe utility, 161, 166
WSDL (Web Service Descriptor Language) file,
  159–62, *162*
www.introducingmicrosoft.net, 10, 25, 154, 181

www.msdn.microsoft.com/net, 25
www.passport.com, 132

X

XML (Extensible Markup Language)
  configuration files, 86, 89, 114, 131, 159–62,
    162
  Web Services and, 152–53, *153, 154* (*see*
    also Web Services)

Z

zones, program, 89

David S. Platt

President and founder of Rolling Thunder Computing, David S. Platt teaches programming of .NET at companies all over the world. He is the author of five previous books on programming in Windows, most recently *Understanding COM+* (Microsoft Press, 1999), which was at one point outselling Tom Clancy's *Every Man a Tiger* on Amazon.com. (That shows you what kind of geeks buy their books there.) He is also a frequent contributor to *MSDN Magazine*.

Dave holds a master of engineering degree from Dartmouth College. When he stops working, he spends his free time working some more. He wonders whether he should tape down two of his daughter's fingers so that she can learn how to count in octal. He lives in Ipswich, Massachusetts, and can be contacted at *www.rollthunder.com*.

The manuscript for this book was prepared and submitted to Microsoft Press in electronic form. Text files were prepared using Microsoft Word 2000. Pages were composed by Microsoft Press using Adobe PageMaker 6.52 for Windows, with text in Optima and display type in Optima Bold. Composed pages were delivered to the printer as electronic prepress files.

Cover Graphic Designer
Methodologie, Inc.

Interior Graphic Artist
James D. Kramer

Principal Compositor
Dan Latimer

Principal Copy Editor
Patricia Masserman

Indexer
**Shane-Armstrong
Information Systems**

The Anvil

The anvil is used as a platform for shaping metal. The first metals to be shaped, copper and bronze, were fashioned on anvils of flat stone. As tools evolved, stone anvils were replaced by larger, cast-bronze models with the characteristic conical break, or horn, at one end, which is used for hammering curved pieces of metal. The modern anvil is constructed of several iron pieces welded together, usually either wrought iron or cast iron, with a flat working surface of hardened steel. The anvil on the cover of this book is a bench anvil; floor-standing anvils are used when shaping large pieces of metal.

Tools are central to the progress of the human race. Humans are adept at building and using tools to accomplish important (and unimportant) tasks. Software is among the most powerful of tools moving humanity to new frontiers. Microsoft is proud to create tools used by millions worldwide and to contribute to this continuing innovation.

Practical strategies and a proven model for developing *great teams* and world-class software

UNDER PRESSURE AND ON TIME

Microsoft

Practical strategies and a proven model for developing great teams and world-class software

Ed Sullivan
Foreward by John Robbins

✓ Best Practices

U.S.A.   **$29.99**
Canada $43.99
ISBN: 0-7356-1184-X

How do you hire—and keep—the best software engineers in the business? What real-world practices will motivate a team to produce excellent results? From startups to major corporations, virtually every development organization struggles with these questions as they attempt to ship great software on time. In UNDER PRESSURE AND ON TIME, respected industry veteran Ed Sullivan shares the critical insights and hard-learned lessons gained from his award-winning, 17-year career in software development. He describes a proven model for creating, directing, and growing a successful development team, and he reveals key secrets and essential "how-to" techniques, about which frustratingly little has been written—until now. This book digs deeper than other project management books to deliver the fire-tested practices and gritty details— direct from the trenches—that will help you assemble a great development team and lead it to ship world-class software.

Microsoft®

mspress.microsoft.com

Get developer-to-developer *insights* for building and customizing Office XP solutions!

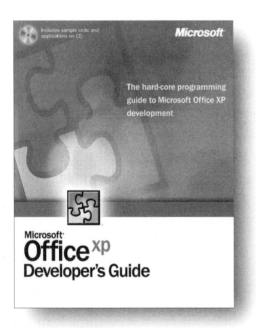

U.S.A. **$49.99**
Canada $72.99
ISBN: 0-7356-1242-0

Exploit the powerful programmability in Microsoft® Office XP with authoritative information straight from the Office XP development team. This hard-core programming reference comes packed with practical resources to help you maximize your productivity with Microsoft Office Developer. You get both design and coding examples that take advantage of the COM interfaces exposed by Office XP. Use this incisive coverage to build on what you know and to accomplish everything from automating simple tasks to creating complex vertical-market applications. And the companion CD-ROM contains procedure code you can use right now—helping you to focus your creativity on designing solutions, rather than on building rudimentary code. It's everything you need to create better business solutions, faster!

***Microsoft*®**

mspress.microsoft.com

Get a **Free**
e-mail newsletter, updates,
special offers, links to related books,
and more when you

register on line!

Register your Microsoft Press® title on our Web site and you'll get
a FREE subscription to our e-mail newsletter, *Microsoft Press Book
Connections.* You'll find out about newly released and upcoming books
and learning tools, online events, software downloads, special offers
and coupons for Microsoft Press customers, and information about
major Microsoft® product releases. You can also read useful additional
information about all the titles we publish, such as detailed book
descriptions, tables of contents and indexes, sample chapters, links to
related books and book series, author biographies, and reviews by other
customers.

Registration is easy. Just visit this Web
page and fill in your information:

http://mspress.microsoft.com/register

Microsoft